D0960747

LESSONS FROM THE EDGE

Praise for *Lessons from the Edge*

"It's what you learn after you know it all, that counts the most."

—George A. Cohon, Founder & Senior Chairman
McDonald's Restaurants of Canada and McDonald's Russia

"*Lessons from the Edge* is an extraordinary series of true encounters!
This book is not a book, but an experience. For every entrepreneur or
aspiring entrepreneur, this book will keep you awake, and
you will learn from it"

—David Irvin, Chairman of The Icehouse, Genesis Research and
Development Corporation, and Cable Bay Wines

"Business is the ultimate competitive challenge. *Lessons from the Edge*
tells the true stories of victories and challenges in business.
Page after page you'll read about the passion, courage, persistence,
and vision—all essential elements of success. *Lessons from the Edge* helps
you navigate through the rough seas of business."

—Philippe Kahn, CEO LightSurf Technologies, Inc. and Pegasus Racing

"*Lessons from the Edge* is an amazing book. It provides years of real life
experience distilled into a few hours of reading."

—Marshall Goldsmith, Executive Coach,
Founding Director of the Alliance for Strategic Leadership,
and author of Global Leadership the Next Generation

"The struggles with edgeship, so clearly described in *Lessons from the Edge*,
provide important guidance for aspiring entrepreneurs. Although different
crises were confronted in different ways, success always required focused
drive, stubborn persistence and the courage to risk being wrong—traits
that every one of the men and women profiled in this inspiring book
demonstrate time and time again."

—Chuck Robinson, President, M Ship Co.,
member Nike Board of Directors, and
former Deputy Secretary of State

"A terrific read, full of drama, striving and learning that shows
what it really takes to build a successful company."

—Ray Smilor, Author, Daring Visionaries and President, Beyster Institute

"*Lessons from the Edge* has successfully transformed peer to
peer learning to the written word. CEO's, presidents and business owners
will recognize its true value right away!"

—Mark Lange, Executive Director, Edward Lowe Foundation

"This great book graphically describes the human leadership qualities
demonstrated by entrepreneurs. It gives vivid examples of how these leaders
have to generate a vision, mobilize resources, and deal with the inevitable
setbacks of building a company."

—Sir Paul Judge, Chairman of the British–North American Committee, Chairman-Elect of
the Royal Society of Arts, President of the Association of MBAs, Vice President of the
Marketing Council, and a Trustee of the American Management Association

Lessons from the Edge

SURVIVAL SKILLS FOR STARTING AND GROWING A COMPANY

JANA MATTHEWS
JEFF DENNIS

WITH PETER ECONOMY

OXFORD
UNIVERSITY PRESS
2003

OXFORD
UNIVERSITY PRESS

Oxford   New York
Auckland   Bangkok   Buenos Aires   Cape Town   Chennai
Dar es Salaam   Delhi   Hong Kong   Istanbul   Karachi   Kolkata
Kuala Lumpur   Madrid   Melbourne   Mexico City   Mumbai   Nairobi
SãoPaulo   Shanghai   Taipei   Tokyo   Toronto

Copyright © 2003 by Jana Matthews and Jeff Dennis

Published by Oxford University Press, Inc.
198 Madison Avenue, New York, New York 10016

www.oup.com

Oxford is a registered trademark of Oxford University Press

All rights reserved. No part of this publication may be reproduced, stored in a retrieval system,
or transmitted, in any form or by any means, electronic, mechanical, photocopying, recording,
or otherwise, without the prior permission of Oxford University Press.

Library of Congress Cataloging-in-Publication Data

Matthews, Jana B.
    Lessons from the edge : survival skills for starting and growing a company /
by Jana Matthews, Jeff Dennis, with Peter Economy.
        p.   cm.
    ISBN 0-19-516825-9 (cloth : alk. paper)
    1. New business enterprises. 2. Entrepreneurship. 3. Management.
I. Dennis, Jeff. II. Economy, Peter. III. Title.
HD62.5 .M366 2003
658.1'142—dc21   2003007970
Rev.

9 8 7 6 5 4 3 2 1
Printed in the United States of America
on acid-free paper

≈ Contents ≈

Jana Matthews
To Chuck and Carolyn, my husband and daughter,
who provided unconditional love and support
to me on my entrepreneurial journey.

Jeff Dennis
To the most important people in my life—
Lori, Matt, and Allie.

≈ Acknowledgments ≈

We are grateful to the members of the Young Entrepreneurs Organization (YEO) and its graduate organization, the World Entrepreneurs Organization (WEO) who encouraged us to write this book. The YEO/WEO culture emphasizes sharing and caring for each other. Members are taught a protocol for sharing their current problems and helping each other avoid – or recover – from the edge.

"Lessons from the Edge" sessions are always the highest rated events at YEO's international conferences. Members crowd into the room and sit on the "edge" of their seats as they listen to peers tell personal and business stories and the lessons they have learned. Since entrepreneurs, by definition, are pushing the envelope, those in the audience are usually close to the "edge" themselves, so they can relate to the candor and emotions of their peers.

When they heard we were writing this book, over 150 entrepreneurs volunteered to share their stories and lessons with us, and many did so in graphic detail! We are honored that they trusted us with their stories, and we're sorry we are not able to acknowledge them all, by name. We are very grateful that they were willing to help us help other entrepreneurs learn how to stay away from the "edge."

We also want to thank Brien Biondi, CEO of YEO/WEO, Mohamed Fathelbab, former Executive Director of YEO, and Gordon Mawhinney, Sean Magennis, and Vijay Tirathrai who were each president of YEO/WEO during the years it took us to write and publish this book. Without your support, this book might not have gotten off the ground.

The Kauffman Foundation provided support for the development and writing of this book. Kate Pope Hodel never doubted there would be a strong demand for a book like this. Our research indicated that entrepreneurs learn from stories and prefer to learn from each other. We had developed frameworks describing what entrepreneurs need to know to manage growth. The stories and lessons in this book certainly validate those frameworks. In addition to Kate, we also want to thank John Tyler, Marianne Hudson, Cindy White, and Tom Phillips for helping us "keep the faith" and encouraging us to press ahead with this book.

We would like to thank Peter Economy for his invaluable work on the book. Peter interviewed over 100 entrepreneurs for *Lessons From The Edge*, and then helped us shape the stories in the book from hundreds of pages of transcripts.

We also want to recognize the contributions of Mark Butler, Content Evangelist at Boulder Quantum Ventures. Thanks, Mark, for sharing our vision and working with us to develop a book that is especially designed for entrepreneurs.

Jeff wants to acknowledge the members of his YEO Forum who were always there for him, through thick and thin, especially Murray Kline, Ken Priestman, Rob Pal and Lorne Merkur. In addition, he feels blessed to have two great business partners, Grant Roebuck and Frank Jacobs. Their brotherhood of experience has created a bond that transcends business.

Jana's daughter Carolyn, and Jeff's children, Matt and Allie, know what it's like to have a parent who is an entrepreneur. They have experienced the highs and lows of business with us. They have celebrated success, provided comfort when we were near the "edge," and watched us re-invent our companies. They now understand what's required to succeed. We are very grateful for their love and support. We also want to thank other members of our families who helped us survive the ups and downs of business and our personal "edge" experiences. Jeff appreciates the love and support that his parents David and Harriet Dennis have provided. They have always been there for him.

We want to thank our agent, Jim Levine, as well as Martha Cooley, Frank Fusco, Dino Battista and the whole team at Oxford University Press. It's a pleasure to work with such professional people who really know their trade.

Finally, and perhaps most importantly, we want to acknowledge the support and love of our spouses, Chuck and Lori. Being the spouse of an entrepreneur is a difficult role. He or she shares all of the risks of entrepreneurship, without having much control. Chuck has been patient, wise, and optimistic. Lori has been the ideal entrepreneurial spouse, providing support and encouragement, while at the same time closing ranks when circumstances required. Both have been true partners, and we consider ourselves fortunate, indeed, to be married to them.

Jana Matthews
Boulder, Colorado
jana.matthews@BoulderQV.com

Jeff Dennis
Toronto, Canada
jmdennis@attcanada.ca

≈ Preface ≈

Two years ago, Jana Matthews and Jeff Dennis announced their plans to write a book called Lessons from the Edge, patterned after an unique Young Entrepreneurs' Organization (YEO) program of the same name. And now, you are holding the results of their efforts: true stories about business owners who faced failure and found a way to succeed.

While YEO and its alumni organization, World Entrepreneurs' Organization (WEO) always have knowledgeable outside experts speaking at their conferences, the most popular sessions are the ones where members tell their own stories. These entrepreneurs talk openly and honestly about what they did wrong—or what went wrong—in their company.

These sessions are more than just "scary campfire stories." Presenters must describe what steps they took to recover from the incident—and what they personally learned from that experience. These are very powerful sessions. Everyone in attendance learns what to do, what not to do, and how to recover from disasters that may be awaiting them. And they learn it from a true peer who faced the edge and survived.

The response of the audience varies. Some people listen, others take notes. But a few jump up, leave the room, and call the office because they realize that they are about to experience the same problems!

This book is a treasure trove of powerful stories and lessons that are applicable to every company. We know you will enjoy the stories, and we hope you will benefit from the real-life lessons learned from your peers. You may find yourself taking notes on the lessons. Or you may throw down the book and rush to action when you suddenly realize you're about to experience some of these same disasters. While this book won't automatically keep you from the edge, you'll be able to recognize when you're getting close, and you'll be armed with tactics and strategies to recover.

Jana Matthews and Jeff Dennis aren't just experts on entrepreneurs . . . they **are** entrepreneurs. They have taken on a role that YEO applauds: entrepreneurs helping their peers. You will hear their own stories in the book in addition to the more than 50 entrepreneurs featured within.

In addition to collecting and analyzing the many stories in the book, Jana and Jeff have been long-time allies of our organization. Jana first began working with YEO through the Ewing Marion Kauffman Foundation's work with entrepreneurs, and continues today with her development of YEO educational programs. Jeff is the co-founder of the Toronto chapter, an international board member during the early years of YEO, and a presenter and moderator of Lessons from the Edge sessions at YEO events.

We are proud that so many members of Young Entrepreneurs' Organization and World Entrepreneurs' Organization have shared their stories and offered their lessons. We hope this book will enable other entrepreneurs to avoid the edge and find both business and personal success.

Sean Magennis, President 2002/2003
Vijay Tirathrai, President 2004/2005
Young Entrepreneurs' Organization
World Entrepreneurs' Organization

LESSONS FROM THE EDGE

≈ Introduction ≈

The edge. Those two words evoke fear and excitement: fear of falling and excitement from the rush of adrenaline. But entrepreneurs who have created successful businesses and then lost them (or almost lost them) know the edge is not a good place to be. In fact, they'd do almost anything to avoid the edge, if they only knew how. And for most entrepreneurs and business owners, the thought of losing the companies that they built with years of blood, sweat, and tears gives them nightmares.

But there's good news. It is possible to avoid the edge without having to experience it yourself—if you can learn from other people's mistakes and identify what pushed them to their edge. The trick is to be able to re-live the experiences of others, understand what they did right and wrong, and discover what they did to fix the problem. But re-living the experiences of others can also be scary. You can find your self face-to-face with the realization that you and your company are very close to the same edge! And that can be frightening if you don't have the knowledge and experience to know how to move away from the edge and survive.

All entrepreneurs and business owners have wished, at one time or another, for a mentor and a guide, a Yoda who will prepare them for what lies ahead and teach them how to respond to danger. While we cannot claim to be Yoda, we have created a book that can serve as your mentor and guide.

The Survivors of the "Edge"

Lessons from the Edge contains more than 50 stories of entrepreneurs who made mistakes in leadership, in financing their growth, in the people they chose as partners and employees, and in how they managed their partnerships, their employees, and their company. It's about people who didn't really know what they had to do or how they needed to change as the company grew. It's about people who never realized they were on the edge until disaster struck, and then weren't sure how to survive—or recover.

We interviewed more than 100 entrepreneurs who volunteered to share their "Lessons from the Edge" stories with us. These interviews produced more than 400 pages of transcripts—enough content for several books!

Most of the entrepreneurs you will meet are profiled in full in one of five sections: Leadership, People, Partnerships, Money, and Personal Issues. Some of those entrepreneurs will pop up in other sections of the book when an element of their story helps to enhance another individual's experience. You will also briefly meet a handful of entrepreneurs who, due to space constraints, could not be featured in full but whose insights were too valuable to overlook.

As we worked through the interviews, we found some stories that were long on painful details and short on self-reflection and learning. A few were clearly mistakes of the heart or bad judgment calls. But most were "spot on" stories about what you need to know to manage growth. We purposely chose the stories and lessons that represent issues and problems faced by the majority of entrepreneurs and company owners. Taken together, they comprise a unique reservoir of wisdom.

All the entrepreneurs in our sample believe that by sharing what they learned at the "School of Hard Knocks," they can help the next generation of entrepreneurs and business owners avoid these same mistakes. They represent a cross section of companies in all kinds of industries. Most of them are members of Young Entrepreneurs' Organization (YEO) or World Entrepreneurs' Organization (WEO). All have revenues over $1 million per year and are younger than 45. Most are from North America, although we also have stories from entrepreneurs in Asia and Europe.

Avoiding the Edge

This book is not just a collection of anecdotes from entrepreneurs willing to "tell all." It's grounded in eight years of research done at the Kauffman Foundation about what entrepreneurs need to know to grow companies, and it builds on frameworks outlined in other books we have written that address how to manage growth.*

Some ask us, "Is it really possible to avoid the edge?" The answer is "yes!" That's exactly why we wrote this book—so entrepreneurs and business owners everywhere could get smarter about building and growing companies, and so they wouldn't have to continue making the same mistakes over again. By the end of this book, you should be able to recognize the red flags and the warning signs. You'll have scenarios, alternatives, plans, and strategies that will help you avoid, navigate, and hopefully survive the edge. And although we haven't included every problem or issue you'll ever face, we've identified the set of issues that creates most of the problems for anyone trying to grow a company. We can't promise that this book will keep you from the edge, but we are sure you will be much better prepared if you find yourself there.

If you want to avoid the edge—now or in the future—here are a few things you need to do. First, you need to understand the kinds of issues that can send you to the edge. You have to recognize the warning signs when you're on the edge. You need to know what corrective action to take to get off the edge. And you must understand what changes are required—in your company, your systems, and your leadership—so you can avoid that particular edge in the future.

---

*See *Leading at the Speed of Growth: Journey from Entrepreneur to CEO* (Hungry Minds/Wiley, 2001) and *Building the Awesome Organization: Six Components that Drive Entrepreneurial Growth* (Wiley, 2002), which Jana Matthews co-authored with Katherine Catlin.

Last, after you've had a "near death" experience at the edge, it's important to know how to move on beyond the fear and emotions of that incident. That can be difficult to do, especially if the business failed, but it's essential to learn how to let go and move on. Our entrepreneurs will share how they did that.

In short, this book contains amazing accounts of entrepreneurs who have overcome adversity, who persisted, who had the courage of their convictions, who survived, and who are now much wiser because of their "edge" experiences. The book demonstrates the triumph of the spirit of entrepreneurs everywhere.

The Authors' Personal Tales from the Edge

The authors have learned their own painful lessons of starting and building a business from scratch. We too know what it's like to peer over the edge of disaster, face the challenge, then move on.

Jana's Story

Jana Matthews is a born entrepreneur. Her journey began when her father, aged 55, started his own company. Every summer, he took Jana along on sales calls and taught her important lessons about honesty, trustworthiness, understanding customers' needs, selling high-quality products, and the principles of good customer service.

Because her family was always short on money, Jana had to work her way through college. She went to Earlham College on a series of scholarships and work grants, held down a part-time job, majored in English, and got a special scholarship to do a junior year abroad at the University of London, Berkbeck College. Jana went to graduate school at Yale, taught school, and then moved into college and university administration. She did management consulting for Arthur D. Little (where she met her husband, Dr. Charles Halbower), then spent four years on a doctorate at Harvard. Several years after Chuck and Jana moved to Boulder, Colorado, they decided to create their own company, M&H Group, Inc.

To finance M&H Group, Jana and Chuck—like so many other entrepreneurs—cashed in their savings, borrowed on their life insurance policies, maxed out their credit cards, and pledged their house to get a line of credit from the bank. The company's focus was entrepreneurship, technology-based economic development, university-industry partnerships, and technology transfer. They added staff, opened an office in the Washington, D.C., area, shared equity with a partner, and were soon on their way.

Then disaster struck.

Jana's mother died, the IRS threatened her father (who had stopped paying his income taxes several years before) with jail, she was diagnosed with breast cancer, and her D.C. partner tried to take over the company when Jana's attention was focused elsewhere. Any one of those factors could have put the company on the edge. All four together created huge problems.

Jana managed to reconstruct five years of her father's taxes, wrap up her mother's estate, survive surgery and six months of chemotherapy, and negotiate a "departure" of the D.C. partner with help from her board. It was a very tough year, and the business slowly spiraled downward. As contracts became more difficult to find, Jana began to wonder if they would survive. Then, out of the blue, *Business Week* magazine did a cover story on hot spots for growth in the United States, and wrote that M&H Group was one of only three companies that really understood technology-based economic development. The phones began to ring again.

The success of M&H Group resulted in an eight-year stint with the Kansas City–based Ewing Marion Kauffman Foundation, where Jana helped to build their new Center for Entrepreneurial Leadership and did several years of research on what entrepreneurs need to know to manage growth. But Jana was bitten by the entrepreneurial bug once again, and in 2000 she moved back to Boulder, founding Boulder Quantum Ventures with the intent of helping other entrepreneurs learn what she had learned about managing growth. Based on what she now knew, she was convinced she would do it right this time. First she developed the company vision, mission, and business plan, and then Jana hired a chief operating officer with potential to move up to chief executive officer. She hired awesome people and garnered terrific contracts. Things were going great.

And then, September 11 came along. Jana was in England and couldn't get home for a week. Her staff desperately needed her leadership in this dark hour—telephone and e-mail just weren't enough. With each passing day, another contract was canceled, and the company's business plan began to disintegrate. Jana was forced to lay off her entire staff, take a huge loss, go back to the drawing board and reinvent the company. Once again she tapped into her retirement plans, borrowed from friends, and took out a second mortgage; Chuck agreed to pledge their house to get a line of credit and to borrow on their life insurance policies and credit cards.

For Jana, writing this book has given her the courage to carry on, to come back from the edge, and to make Boulder Quantum Ventures a success. She's had to change her plan and her strategy, let go of the past, and focus on the future. But all these experiences Jana has had as an entrepreneur, her work at Kauffman, and her work with hundreds of other entrepreneurs have enabled Jana to learn what entrepreneurs need to know to manage growth and what they need to do to unlock their growth potential. That knowledge and wisdom is reflected in this book.

Jeff's Story

Co-author Jeff Dennis is one of the entrepreneurs who has been the "poster boy" for *Lessons from the Edge*. Jana and Jeff go way back, having worked together on several projects involving the Young Entrepreneurs' Organization and the Kauffman Center.

Jeff's journey to the edge and back again is a classic "riches-to-rags-to-riches" saga. Born into a life of privilege—private schools, summer camps, and country clubs—Jeff was afforded the finest education money could buy, including Canada's prestigious Upper Canada College and Brown University. The scion of a well-known Toronto real estate family, Jeff obtained his law degree from the University of Western Ontario and was being groomed to lead the family business.

Following the entrepreneurial call, Jeff soon found himself in a real estate syndication business with several partners—including law school classmate Grant Roebuck—riding high on one of the hottest real estate markets of all time. Unfortunately, after a period of early success, the Canadian real estate bubble burst in 1991, bringing Jeff's young business to a grinding halt. The crash in the real estate market didn't just wreck Jeff's business; it wiped out his family's real estate fortune as well. With his wife Lori and two young children to support, Jeff soon found himself more than $1 million in debt and stuck with a fast-depreciating house that had cost him more than $1.5 million only a few months before.

Jeff, at age 31, wasn't just looking over the edge and into the abyss; he was falling in.

Jeff and Lori sold their house—renting a home in a modest neighborhood noted for having good public schools—and Lori went back to work, earning enough money to provide the basic necessities for the family. Things were so bad that Jeff couldn't even afford the gas to drive to work each day, let alone the cost of parking. Afraid he would not be able to make it on his own, Jeff seriously considered taking a job at a law firm. Just when it looked as though Jeff would have to give up his dreams, his partner Grant gave him some sage advice: "You must be on the track in order to be hit by the train." In other words, if they were going to succeed, they would have to somehow figure out how to stay in business long enough to find the opportunities that were out there waiting for them.

This was a turning point in Jeff's life.

So, how were Jeff and his partner going to get back on the track, and then stay on it? First, they had to reinvent themselves. When they started their real estate syndication business, Jeff and Grant considered themselves real estate guys. Now—with the real estate market in the tank—they realized that they were not in the real estate business; their business was actually creating financial products and raising money.

The second step was therefore to find their next commodity for raising money. Jeff and Grant discovered that the Canadian government had passed legislation to encourage the development of home-grown Canadian culture—specifically, Canadian film and television productions. Bringing in a new partner—Frank Jacobs, they shifted gears, reinvented the business, and began selling tax sheltered investments in Canadian film and television productions.

The team moved forward quickly. The company's first deal was small—$3.3 million, which they completed in less than 30 days. But over the next eight years, Jeff and his partners did more than $1.5 billion in business, averaging just under $200 million a year. They sold their business in 2001 and never looked back.

For Jeff, writing this book has helped him realize what he learned and why he was able to bounce back from setback after setback—stronger each time. His most important lesson is the value of a strong support network: business partners who freely extended their loyalty, experience, love, and support; a loving wife who pitched in when Jeff desperately needed her and who has been by his side every step of the way; and an organization of peers—the Young Entrepreneurs Organization (YEO), specifically his YEO Forum—who were available whenever he needed to discuss personal and business issues on a highly confidential basis. Jeff has heard each of his Forum members' lessons from the edge, and they have heard his. He and his YEO Forum helped each other the same way this book can help you: provide warnings, give guidance, suggest some options, bulletproof strategies, and provide moral and emotional support.

The Courage of the Entrepreneur

What separates entrepreneurs from other businesspeople? In two words, courage and persistence.

They have the courage to try to build a business in spite of the financial risk, the nay-sayers and pessimists who warn it can't be done, and the giant corporations or entrenched technology with which they have to compete.

It's not about the money. Money is a way to keep score, but very few entrepreneurs do what they do to "get rich." They are driven to do something that has never been done before—to create something new, to capitalize on a new opportunity. They also have a high need to be self-reliant and to determine their own path in life. They are inspired, they are creative, they have a compelling vision, they are courageous, and they are persistent—so persistent that they are often able to introduce new products and services that change the world.

The School of Hard Knocks

Unfortunately, there aren't a lot of resources that help entrepreneurs learn what is required to grow a successful company. You can buy a book on how to read a balance sheet, you can take a course on how to manage people, you can go to a Web site that lists business opportunities—but none of these will give you what you really need. Real lessons from real entrepreneurs—men and women who walk a tightrope without a safety net, day in and day out—are few and far between. Despite the increasing number of entrepreneurship programs at colleges and universities, most entrepreneurs still learn their lessons the old-fashioned way: through the School of Hard Knocks.

In the stories that follow, you'll have a unique opportunity to view the world through the eyes of many different entrepreneurs—all of whom are graduates of that school. Each of them risked everything to build his or her business. You'll experience the overwhelming exhilaration of their success, and the depth of their despair when things go wrong. You'll walk in their shoes and share their excitement, their optimism, their loneliness, their triumphs, and their failures.

This book will enable you to learn real-world lessons that will be immediately useful in your own business and personal life. These entrepreneurs have shared their experience for one reason: They want you to learn from their mistakes so you won't have to make them yourself.

Navigating the Lessons

We have thought a lot about how you can use this book most effectively. If you have a problem that needs to be solved now or are worried about a problem that's waiting in the wings, you can use the Table of Contents and turn right to the story that addresses your issues. For example, if you and your business partner are having problems, or you need to hire a new CEO to take over day-to-day operations of your company, or you aren't sure whether you have systems in place that could detect embezzlement, you can turn right to those stories. On the other hand, if you want to read the book from cover to cover (and we promise that it will be difficult to put down), *Lessons from the Edge* has been organized into five sections.

- Leadership. Leadership is critical to the growth and development of a successful company—regardless of whether it's a for-profit, or not-for-profit company. Effective, inspired leaders can lead employees to do truly great things; poor leadership can decimate a company. No entrepreneur wants to be a poor leader; but too often he or she just doesn't know how to lead. Our stories focus on the roles and responsibilities of the leader, how those roles change as the company grows, and the importance of vision, mission, communication, delegation, a good top team, hiring great people, planning, and anticipating problems.

- **People.** In this section, we present stories focused on the company's second most critical resource: its people. Many entrepreneurs don't know how to hire the right people, what to look for, or how to manage them once they are hired. Large corporations recognize the importance of people skills in their leaders and managers. When entrepreneurs start a company, they have to do it all—make the coffee, sign the checks, design the product, sell to the customers, and negotiate the bank loan. However, their ability to hire good people who can help the company grow—and then delegate to them, build a team, and keep everyone aligned—will be the secret to their success. Our stories and lessons will help you understand what to look for, and how to hire, manage, and lead people to achieve great things. After reading the stories you'll be a lot smarter about what to do—and what not to do.

- **Partnerships.** Here, we explore the upside—and the downside—of partnerships. Many companies are started by two friends or family members without much thought or planning. You think it's more fun to have a partner—and you may think you are sharing the risks by having a partner—but if you choose the wrong partner or the partnership goes sour, you substantially compound your own risk. Each partner needs to contribute something to the business—hopefully something that the other partner does not have in the way of talents, skills, contacts, and resources. Also, partnerships need to be built on respect and affection. It's important to go in with your eyes wide open. Check out whether you share the same goals for the business, and plan ahead for changes that are likely to occur. Good partnerships can turn an ordinary business into a roaring success. Bad partnerships can ruin even the best business, taking the hopes and the dreams (and often the financial security) of the founder along with it. As our stories and lessons will show, partnerships are like marriages—easy to get into, very hard and painful to get out of. After reading this section, you'll have a better road map of what to do to make a partnership successful.

- **Money.** The section on money addresses some of the problems that occur when entrepreneurs don't understand cash flow, don't have good financial systems, and don't bother to watch the numbers and ask questions. Having a positive—and strong—cash flow is essential to the long-term health of every business. Do you understand how money flows through your company? Are there enough new orders coming in to support future growth? Are customers paying their bills on time? Is your burn rate out of control? Are you managing your relationships with your banker? Will the bank extend your line of credit even though your financials are not as good as you had hoped? Can you meet payroll next week? It takes money to make money, and if you're not making enough of it, your business may be closer to the edge than you think. In this section we look at many lessons learned—about financing growth, dealing with banks and venture capitalists, and what happens when you don't have good financial systems in place.

- **Personal Issues**. Finally, we look at the personal issues, the stresses and strains of being an entrepreneur. For the entrepreneurs who have dedicated their lives to building a successful company, their business is much more than just dollars and cents: It's a very personal journey. Since the company is, in many ways, an extension of the entrepreneur—the manifestation of hopes and dreams—a "win" can lift your spirits to great heights. But the business can also be a tremendous financial anchor, and failure can take you far into the deepest, darkest emotional abyss you've ever imagined. Some entrepreneurs have lost their businesses and their fortunes—not just once, but several times over the years. Others have lost relationships, friends, family, and those closest to them as they tried to get their business off the ground or keep it afloat. In the end, every entrepreneur, successful or not, comes to realize that there is more to life than business, and that true success requires balancing a strong commitment to work with an equally strong commitment to personal life. The stories in our final section are thoughtful retrospectives of entrepreneurs who share stories that both educate and inspire us all.

If you have only a general idea about the problems you are facing, we suggest you skim the section overviews for a brief summary of the profiles contained within each section. Once you have identified individual profiles that seem to parallel your own issues, turn to those profiles. Each one begins with a listing of pertinent information:

- The entrepreneur's name, title, and company

- The type of business, location, and annual revenues

- The number of employees and years in business

- The "edge"—that is, the challenge that the entrepreneur faced

In addition to telling a story, each profile also includes lessons learned—both from the entrepreneur's perspective and from our perspective as well. You'll also find a handy list of "Top 10 Lessons" at the end of each section, summarizing the most important lessons within that particular group of profiles.

Real People, Real Stories

Because the bad apples get all the press, it's easy to forget that the vast majority of entrepreneurs are trying to build their businesses ethically and honestly. None of the companies in this book are household names. There are no celebrity CEOs in this group, just hard-working, honest men and women who are trying to build companies that will outlive them and provide financial security for themselves and their families, jobs for their employees, and real value to their customers.

We truly believe that entrepreneurs are the real heroes of our economy, the ones who risk it all to build their businesses. While the big companies—the Fortune 500—get most of the media attention, our nation's small businesses create most of our jobs and wealth, and they play an essential role in building our communities. The men and women in this book may not be Wall Street heroes, but they are definitely Main Street heroes. They are our heroes too.

If you're a business owner, CEO, or entrepreneur, if you're married to an entrepreneur, or if you're part of a family of entrepreneurs, or simply thinking about starting your own company, then this book is for you. This is your opportunity to get a behind-the-scenes peek at what really happens inside a fast-growing company, and to get inside the minds of the men and women who have the courage to risk everything in pursuit of their dreams. Learn from the hundreds of mistakes that these business owners made, and be successful sooner without all the psychological and financial pain they had to endure to get where they are today.

As you read through the stories that follow, think about the lessons and ask yourself, *How does this apply in my company? How am I doing? Are there some things in the way that I'm doing business that need to change? Am I getting close to the edge?* It's not our goal to simply entertain you with these stories. The reason we wrote this book is so that you don't make the same mistakes these successful individuals made. If you do find yourself in similar situations, this book provides you with survival strategies for bringing you and your business back from the edge before you have to learn your own lessons the hard way.

If you're not an entrepreneur, you will gain respect and appreciation for the people who try to make something happen out of nothing. If you are an entrepreneur, we want you to know you are not alone. Many other entrepreneurs have experienced what you are going through in your business. They have found themselves in tough situations, have managed to get through to the other side, and have lived to tell about it.

That said, get ready for a jolt of electricity and courage as you read these stories. They are indeed awesome.

≈ Leadership ≈

Section-at-a-Glance

Overview

Individual Profiles

Profile: Ken Wolf
The Edge: Having to pull the plug on a 3 year/$3 million investment, firing 30+ people and nearly losing the company.

Profile: Douglas Mellinger
The Edge: Not managing growth, not bringing in the right people, taking the company public, a coup, and a significant company decline.

Profile: Frank Nemiroff
The Edge: Widespread timecard fraud and employee theft almost destroying the company.

Profile: Marx Acosta-Rubio
The Edge: Fired with no money in the bank, borrowing against mother's life savings to start his company.

Profile: Mark Moses
The Edge: Turncoat employees and changing markets putting the company on the brink of filing Chapter 7 bankruptcy.

Profile: Joshua Schecter
The Edge: Employee problems jeopardizing client relationships; accountability declining as the company grew.

Profile: Bob Kirstiuk
The Edge: Successful company acquired by a dot-com, erasing ten years of equity and almost $50 million in capital.

Profile: Charles Tetrick
The Edge: Partner dying suddenly without a shareholder agreement or contingency plan.

Profile: Anne Bain
The Edge: Father dying suddenly; daughter having to quickly learn the business and run it; clashed with partner about an unclear partnership agreement.

Profile: Kevin Daum
The Edge: Started a second company, lost a lot of money, came close to losing the first company.

Wrap-up

Top Ten Lessons in Leadership

≈ Leadership ≈
Overview

Few entrepreneurs starting their first company really understand what they need to do as leaders of their companies. They may be good at selling, or inventing, or writing software, but creating a vision and mission and a company culture; recruiting, leading, and managing people; securing outside investments; and planning company growth—this is new territory for most of them. To make matters more confusing, the roles and responsibilities of the leader change as the company grows and develops. As one entrepreneur, chief executive officer (CEO) of a growing company, said, "Just when you get good at something, you discover it's the wrong thing to be doing!" The very behaviors and habit patterns that lead to success in one stage of growth can contribute to failure in the next.

Unfortunately, some CEOs focus too much on leadership style and how they look and act, but are clueless about what they are supposed to do as leaders. If one message comes through loud and clear from the entrepreneurs interviewed for this book, it is this: *In order to keep your company away from the edge—or rescue it if it's at the brink—you need to understand the roles and responsibilities of a leader.*

In this section, you'll read the stories of a number of entrepreneurs who learned their leadership lessons the hard way. Ken Wolf of Revelwood, Inc., found out that one of the roles of the leader is to help the company stay focused on its goals. Losing focus resulted in the loss of millions of dollars to him and his partners, and almost cost him the company.

Frank Nemiroff of Nemco Food Products discovered that his employees were stealing and tampering with time clocks. But rather than firing everyone, he recognized that he had failed to address the needs of the organization—one of the prime responsibilities of the leader. He had not created the vision, mission, values, processes, the systems, and financial controls that an organization needs to function properly.

On the other hand, Damon Gersh (whom you will meet in the People section of the book) did a great job of preparing his company for something he had never imagined: the incredible challenges of the September 11th tragedy. His leadership enabled the company to move quickly, perform effectively, and capitalize on an unparalleled opportunity for growth.

You'll meet many more entrepreneurs who learned just how critical leadership was to the success—or failure—of their companies. Without knowing it, they took their companies to the brink, and then some. Most companies were able to recover from their near disaster, but some weren't and slipped over the edge.

So what is the role of the leader? Damon Gersh said it well. The leader's job is:

> to set the tone and prioritize—to identify what's important for the company, to clarify vision, direction, and values. I empowered people within the organization and brought on the best people I could get. I gave them guidelines, held them accountable, let them exercise their creativity and bring their experience to the table. I trusted them to use the guidelines to make important decisions.

As you read this section, think about how the roles and responsibilities of the leaders changed: What did these CEOs do in the early days at their company that no longer worked when their companies were in high-growth mode? Note how their roles and responsibilities changed each time the company moved from one stage to the next. For example, those who were very hands-on and did everything in the beginning found they needed to learn to delegate and be less opportunity driven as the company grew. They had to learn to choose among opportunities and focus the company. As the company moved into rapid growth, they had to recruit a top team, coach them, get them to plan and function as a team, and even reinvent the company.

Jeffrey Behrens, president of The Telluride Group, a Massachusetts-based company specializing in information technology (IT) outsourcing, said it well:

> Whatever lessons you learn at any stage are often completely inappropriate for the next stage. The rules change. The organizational dynamics, the structure, the demands, your role, job description—everything changes at each stage. At start-up, you have to do everything. But at my stage—30 people, trying to get to 50—the less I do, the better job I'm doing. If your hands are involved in too much, it's a really bad sign. You're not developing leadership; you're not developing entrepreneurship in the folks around you. You're holding the organization back.

Unfortunately, it is hard for some entrepreneurs to let go. Some never do. The result? They get stuck in the start-up stage which means the company is totally dependent on them; they become the bottleneck, and the company never meets its revenue potential. In some cases, it fails. Says Joshua Schechter, president and co-founder of Online Business Services, Inc.:

> I think entrepreneurs are pigheaded in general. They want to do everything themselves. They've always done it that way. They're good at spinning plates. They can stand on one foot and use two hands and their other foot to spin three plates, but when one of those plates begins to wobble, they are afraid to ask somebody to help. They'll just let the plate fall and concentrate on the other two plates. But if you want to grow, you reach a point where you can't spin any more plates and you have to turn over the reins to someone else . . . you have to get help.

If you want employees to take on the roles you played when you founded the company, one of your roles as leader is to create a vision for the people in your company, a vision that inspires them to take action. Like the captain of a ship, the leader sets the course, and the team pulls together to get there. Marx Acosta-Rubio, president of One Stop Shop, a computer supplies wholesaler, shares his lessons learned:

> You have to paint the vision for the people who come to work for you. People see themselves not for what they are, but for less than what they are. They have a lot more talent that they don't recognize because there's nobody there to push them and to persuade them that they can do it. My employees have to borrow my vision to see further than they can see by themselves.

The stories that follow are all about leadership. The entrepreneurs and CEOs in the stories faced many of the same challenges of growth that you and your company have faced—or will face. So as you read these stories, think about the following questions:

- Are you keeping the company focused, or are you allowing yourself and your employees to get distracted?

- Are you building the foundation for an awesome organization?

- Have you identified the vision, mission, and values and created a reason and purpose for your employees to come to work—other than collecting a paycheck?

- Have you created a culture that supports innovation and personal responsibility, with open communication, where people know what is expected of them, where they work hard, have fun, and think and act like owners?

- Have you hired the right people, do you have them in the right jobs, and have you fired the ones that don't fit with the culture or can't do the work you need them to do?

- Have you developed a plan for growth?

- Have you worked with your top team so they can function as extensions of you, and are you ready for the "big opportunity"?

- Have you identified the Critical Success Factors—the economic drivers and factors that can make or break your company?

- Do you have processes and systems in place that make it easy for people to do their work and enable you to track company performance, identify trouble spots, and anticipate problems?

- Have you identified what personal changes you need to make in order to take the company to its next level of development?

Enjoy these leadership lessons from the edge. As you read these stories, think about what you would have done in these situations, and compare yourself to these company leaders.

Individual Profiles

THE PRICE OF DISTRACTION

Factsheet

Name:	Ken Wolf
Title:	President/CEO
Company:	Revelwood, Inc.
Type of Business:	Software/consulting
Location:	New York, New York
Annual Revenue:	not disclosed
Employees:	12
Years in Business:	Company founded 1995
The Edge:	Having to pull the plug on a 3 year/$3 million investment, firing 30+ people and nearly losing the company.

The Story

When Ken Wolf started his company, he had a clear goal in mind: to start small, steadily build a client base, and then roll out a series of products that would incorporate the knowledge and experience gained from these relationships. But as Wolf soon learned, keeping your eye on the ball—and not being distracted by other balls—can be a major challenge. Lose your focus and watch what you spent years building come crashing down.

Says Wolf, "We started the company as a consulting practice for a reason: we wanted to build up a client base; we wanted to build up our expertise in this market and our knowledge of the market; we wanted to build up a team of people; and we wanted to generate cash flow. We wanted to get to a certain level first before rolling out a product. So, for the first two years or so of the firm's existence, that's what we did. We slowly built up a practice—we hired people, we built up a team of consultants, and we did work.

"About two and a half years into it, my partner and I decided we were ready to begin our product development efforts, and that soon became the focus of the company. We brought in a third partner to head up the entire product development piece. As CEO I focused on marketing, sales, HR [human resources], and my original partner focused on continuing to manage and grow the professional services business. When we started this effort, we were six or seven people. By the summer of 2000, we had almost 40 people. We were starting to fill out the organization, and we were going full steam. We hit the 'Inc. 500' list, and received all sorts of other awards within our industry. Things were looking good.

"But we got sucked into something that we shouldn't have. Our intention was to be a solutions company—in other words, to create a combination of business intelligence and technical components that together form a package that solves a business problem. But when we sat down and looked at the market and asked what tools were available to work with to make this happen, we found they didn't exist. So we said, 'Gee, why don't we build the platform? Why don't we build the tool?' Customers liked the idea, our partners liked the idea, we liked the idea, it made a lot of sense, and so we said, 'Let's do it!'

"But pursuing this distracted us from our core competency. We are good at developing solutions. We understand the customers. We understand their business process. We are not a technology company, and that's what we had to become to do this. We lost sight of who we were and what we were good at.

"But we forged on, and developed the product and started marketing and selling it. For a number of reasons, the whole thing came crashing down, and we had to pull the product from the marketplace. The amount of focus that all three of us, as owners of the company, had to put into the new product launch was so significant that it really took us away from our consulting practice. As a result, our consulting practice didn't grow and thrive as it should have, the management layers were weaker than we had wanted, we weren't focused on improving that, so the practice started to deteriorate. This was a *major* problem because we relied on cash generated from the practice to fund the product development effort.

"We got to a point where we couldn't survive any longer. The practice itself could not fund the efforts of the entire company, and we hit the wall. That began a downward spiral of our company in terms of profits, everything, because everything had become dependent on this big product launch. We had to lay off most of our product development team, most of our marketing team, and move in a different direction. That was the toughest day of my career, by far.

"Out of pocket, directly, we lost somewhere between $2 and $3 million. Indirectly, it's a lot more than that. It's the opportunity cost of me and my partners focusing almost exclusively on the new product launch, rather than focusing on building and growing our practice. That 'distraction' took away our ability to sell more, win more, and solidify client relationships. We had to retrench, go back to our roots, and do what we know best."

Lessons Learned

When companies enter a stage of high growth, it's very easy for the leadership team to lose sight of the company's core competencies and to discount what they do best. There's a temptation to believe that if you're successful in one area, you can be successful in any other area—if you just work at it. In Wolf's case, instead of focusing on their core products and competencies—the very things that had made them successful—they turned to something new: developing the technology tools required to develop the new products. When they were included in several lists of high-growth companies, for example, the Inc. 500 list, they began to inhale their own exhaust and believe they could do it all. Then one morning they woke up, realized they had to pull the plug on the product, fire a lot of people, count up the dollars they lost, recognize the opportunity cost, get back to basics, and rebuild the company.

Says Wolf, "Woody Allen once said, 'Don't underestimate the power of distraction,' and I couldn't agree more. I've learned that you have to be focused, and you have to stay focused.

"Focus is so important; it's so easy to just get sucked into so many different things. You lose focus because you spread yourself too thin—you try to do this, and you try to do that. Why? Because you think it's going to help your company survive and grow, but that's generally not the case at all. It's so important to stay focused on the goal and to understand what your niche is.

"You have to pick your niche, focus on it, hone it, and build on it. But we got distracted and didn't even realize it. We tried to do too many things, and we lost our focus. That, I would say, is my greatest lesson."

RIGHT MOVES, WRONG PEOPLE

Factsheet

Name:	Douglas Mellinger
Title:	Chairman/CEO
Company:	Enherent
Type of Business:	Software Development
Location:	New York, New York
Annual Revenue:	$85 million (peak)
Employees:	850 (peak)
Years in Business:	Company founded 1989
The Edge:	Not managing growth, not bringing in the right people, taking the company public, a coup, and a significant company decline.

The Story

In 1989 with $12,000, Douglas Mellinger founded PRT (now called Enherent), a software development firm. At its peak, revenues were $85 million a year, and the company had operations in several countries and cities. At first, his company grew at an incredibly high rate, but problems were just around the corner.

Says Mellinger, "Our whole idea was to find a need and fill it. I knew I wanted to be in the technology industry, and I knew I wanted to be working with large companies as clients versus small companies. I chose the IT space and went to a group of chief information officers and CEOs of very large companies and asked them what their biggest problems were—their needs; I also asked them to help me think through problems I'd face if I tried to fill those needs. And so I started the company and had great input from some really good mentors and advisers. The company was extremely successful; our first-year sales were just under $500,000. The next year, sales jumped to $2.5 million and then $5.3 million, $8 million, $13 million, and then $20 million.

"We did our first project in India in 1990. We started the process of opening up a company in India in 1993. And then in 1994 we started looking for an alternative to having to go all the way to India, and we opened up an office in Barbados. We were the first company to do what we refer to as 'near shore' development. We raised about $3 million from JP Morgan to open up that facility and then raised another $15 million in 1996 from Prudential and Travelers. We opened up another 50,000 square foot facility in Hartford, Connecticut. In the fall of 1996 we started really rapid growth, and one year later we went public. During that year we grew by about 500 people and went from a $22–23 million company to a $60 million company. And it was just complete mayhem. We grew way, way too fast.

"Toward the end of 1998, I knew that the industry was going to go through further hell because of Y2K, and that by June of '99 people were going to lock down their software. I knew that the industry was going to get completely smashed. When I realized the industry was not going to grow like it had in the past, I decided to leave and do some stuff around the Internet."

While Mellinger's personal decision to move on may have been good for him, it was not a good decision for the company. He had not staffed the company with the right people to carry on after he left. He had hired people who were slowing down progress, and as a result, ultimately ended up exiting his leadership role prematurely because of a hiring choice.

"I made the mistake of hiring people based upon pedigree. I hired this one guy who was a Harvard MBA. He was a big-time head of consulting at one of the Big Five accounting firms. He was the CIO (chief information officer) for one of the biggest management con-sulting firms—a really heavy duty guy. And if you just needed some-one to build a hill, he probably would have been phenomenal. But if you needed someone to create a mountain, he was the wrong per-son. He couldn't do it. This person came in about eight months before our IPO (initial public offering) when I was heavily tied up with the process of going public. I was getting all of my reports, but the reports weren't giving me information about what was really going on in the company; the reports were all based on the kind of momentum that had been built up months ago. I was getting infor-mation from behind the wave rather than ahead of the wave.

"When I went out to recruit a number two for the company, I had the total support of the board. We brought a guy on board in May of '99. We were getting along okay, but he ended up pulling a power play with some of the board members; he wanted to run the whole company earlier than I agreed to. I had set it up so I would stay on into the year 2000. But by the end of June '99, he wanted to take over the company, then and there.

"For the first five minutes I was very upset about it. Then I real-ized I could go on to the next chapter of my life. It turned out to be the greatest thing that happened to me. I stayed on as chairman for another 15 months. I'm just a board member today.

"Unfortunately, the company is now a disaster. After Y2K, the whole industry lost about half its sales. The company went up to $85 million and has been declining ever since."

Lessons Learned

As Doug Mellinger discovered, when a company is growing, it takes a top team of talented and dedicated people who can do more than just keep up; they need to be able to stay ahead of the growth curve. But it's the leader's job to make sure the right people are hired, and Mellinger wasn't always able to bring in those people.

Smart leaders hire other people with leadership skills, with the expectation that they will take on current and future leadership roles, hence freeing the company's CEO to take on new roles and responsibilities. But that can only happen if you hire the right people, and then delegate appropriately. Hiring the wrong people creates more work with fewer results and actually places additional burdens on the CEO instead of removing them.

Says Mellinger, "We hired these guys, and they brought in their people, and they were all alike—and that was a real problem. As a result, we just didn't have the horsepower to bring this company forward—and, in fact, they did humongous damage to the company. Looking back, I should have used a search firm. We didn't do that for many of these positions, and I think it was a mistake. You need to have as broad a pool as possible to pick from, and I think search firms do a very good job of finding people for those very critical positions. Search firms are expensive but I think it's more expensive not to use them. It cost me millions of dollars in severance fees to get rid of the people who weren't performing. And in some cases I should have gotten rid of them sooner.

"I'm not making that mistake with my new company. I've hired the A team from day one. I'm not hiring the B or C team like I did the last time. I've learned you can't grow a company rapidly unless you have the very best team in place."

Doug Mellinger did a lot of things right. He didn't grow a company from $500,000 to $85 million on dumb luck. But as he looks back on his experience, Mellinger realizes that he failed to perform one of the critical roles of the leader: Find the very best people for the job, help them achieve clearly stated goals, train them, coach them, give them opportunities to grow—or, if they don't perform as expected, fire them, if necessary.

STEALING THE COMPANY BLIND

Factsheet

Name:	Frank Nemiroff
Title:	President
Company:	Nemco Food Products
Type of Business:	Restaurant supply
Location:	Vernon, California
Annual Revenue:	$9 million
Employees:	22
Years in Business:	Company founded 1960
The Edge:	Widespread timecard fraud and employee theft almost destroying the company.

The Story

Frank Nemiroff believed that his company was doing well, but he failed to see just how rotten his organization was becoming, at its core. Not only were workers committing timecard fraud but they were stealing products from right under his nose.

Says Nemiroff, "A group of employees figured out how to open up our time clock and reset the hours. The guy who was leaving at 8:00 P.M. would open up the clock and set the clock to 10:00 P.M., punch out, and then reset the clock to the correct time. I was being overcharged countless hours of overtime throughout the entire company. And it wasn't just one or two people; it had become endemic and systemic throughout the organization. Almost every hourly employee in the company was doing timecard fraud.

"At first, I had no idea what was going on. But I began to notice that some of the timecards had some irregularities. My late-night order checking department leaves between 8:00–9:00 P.M.—whenever all the orders are correct. They set the alarm in the area of the warehouse that we operate, so the whole building is alarmed except for this one little area. I don't know why I decided to do this, but I decided to check the alarm settings from the computer log of when the alarm is open and closed.

"I noticed that the alarm would be set at 7:00 P.M., but my guys were punching out at 9:30 P.M. As soon as I saw that, I realized I had a big, big problem."

But that was just the beginning of Nemiroff's problems. "One day, I got a call from my office. One of my drivers reported that the dock manager handed him a rather suspicious looking box and asked him to drop it off in the dock manager's car on his way out to the parking lot. He agreed, but then decided it looked kind of suspicious, so he just drove on, got to his next stop, called the office, and said, 'I've got this box. I don't know what to do with it.'

"I met the driver and we opened up this suspicious looking box. The printing on the box indicated it was dish soap. It had been resealed and packaged up, and the box was so light I knew it couldn't be dish soap. We opened up the box and inside were several cases of cigarettes and cigars. We went to the local police, and we had the dock manager arrested right here, at the office, and taken out in handcuffs."

Despite the huge loss that the timecard fraud and theft was costing his company, Nemiroff decided against firing his entire staff and starting all over again. There was a practical reason: Without employees he would have been hard-pressed to deliver products and services to clients. But there were other reasons. He did not feel it was fair to single out certain employees for punishment when he couldn't decisively prove who else—or how many people— were involved. And he blamed himself for these widespread problems. "I realized that I had fallen asleep at the wheel in terms of the organization's needs. The culture had fallen out of control. We did not have the organization in place."

Nemiroff was convinced that changes could be made, and he quickly brought in outside help. "The first thing I needed to do was to assess my company culture. I did some soul searching about what I wanted the company to look like and where I wanted it to go. The next step was to determine how we were going to get there, and then implement it. I hired a consultant, and we are in the middle of this process now. We've done the culture assessment, figured out what we want, and what the company should look like. Finally, after getting kicked in the ass, I have put together some company values, company purpose, company mission and vision—the kinds of documents we did not have before."

Lessons Learned

When a company is in the start-up phase, the entrepreneur is responsible for everything: product development, sales, purchasing, accounting, and more.

As the company grows and the entrepreneur delegates an increasing proportion of his or her responsibilities to employees, management and financial controls become increasingly important to ensure the ongoing health of the company. One of the responsibilities of the leader is creating the infrastructure (structure, processes, systems, and procedures) that will support growth. Unfortunately Frank Nemiroff had to learn this the hard way.

But there's more to leadership than a good infrastructure. Most first-time entrepreneurs give little attention to issues such as culture, mission, vision, and values, yet these elements are major responsibilities of the leader. Successful entrepreneurs understand the importance of culture and values. A well-defined company culture and a clearly articulated set of values and ethical standards will guide company operations and decision making at all levels of the company. Culture and values start early. Don't just hire people who can perform their jobs; make sure they are also a good match with the values and the culture of the company.

Building a culture begins with communicating the CEO's own beliefs and linking them to the company's mission and vision. Regular communication of a clear consistent message is essential for a growing company.

Says Nemiroff, "When you have a growing company, the organization needs to evolve, and the faster you're growing, the faster it needs to evolve. My greatest lesson learned was to be aware of the organization's needs: It needs structure, systems, processes, accountability, reporting—all of these need to be in place. In my case, they weren't. I was in denial that I needed these things. I don't like this stuff. I would much rather sell product and look at my bottom line.

"But now I understand why it's important to have a company purpose and a company mission. It's what makes the company something more than just a paycheck for the employees. I think employees need to grab onto something that gives them a compelling reason to come to work, like excellence, respect for individuals, differentiating ourselves from our competition, the fact that we are a comfortable workplace and not a sweatshop.

"What made me start thinking about all of this is when I thought, 'Why should my employees care? What do we do here that is of any importance?' Someone who works for the Red Cross or the fire department or Save the Whales—these people have a mission. They get up in the morning knowing that they are trying to make a difference. They have a real purpose. And my company's also got to have a clear mission of what it's about. It's not enough to be putting stuff on trucks and collecting money so we can all pay our rent. There's got to be more to it than that. And it's my job as leader to tell them what that mission is."

As policies and procedures are put into place, it also becomes increasingly important for leaders to hold their employees accountable for results. Says Nemiroff, "I tolerated mediocrity way too long. I had a lot of mediocre people who were just getting by. I'm now putting performance standards in place and holding people accountable. But this is not the kind of stuff I want to do myself. I'm now looking to hire somebody to do it, and hold them accountable."

Frank Nemiroff learned the hard way the importance of building the organization needed to support growth. And he also realized that he had to step up to the plate and lead with a newfound emphasis on mission, vision, culture, and values. His leadership brought his company back from the brink.

YOU GOTTA BELIEVE

Factsheet

Name:	Marx Acosta-Rubio
Title:	President
Company:	One Stop Shop
Type of Business:	Computer supplies
Location:	Tarzana, California
Annual Revenue:	$4 million
Employees:	12
Years in Business:	Company founded 1998
The Edge:	Fired with no money in the bank, borrowing against mother's life savings to start his company.

The Story

After his mentor died, Marx Acosta-Rubio took a long hard look at his own life. He was making good money, but he realized that things like character, integrity, and honesty meant more to him than he had realized. He was thinking through his next steps when word leaked out that he was going to leave. His boss came into his office and promptly fired him. He was married, had a one-year-old baby, and had no money in the bank. He had to move in with his mother.

Acosta-Rubio talked his mother into letting him use her life savings—$77,000—as collateral for a line of credit with a local bank.

He started his computer supplies company in 1998 out of the house. His company did $1 million in sales its very first year. One Stop Shop has since grown to more than $4 million in annual revenues, serving more than 1,000 clients with a staff of 12. But, Acosta-Rubio knows that growth like this doesn't happen in a vacuum. Part of his job as leader is to create a vision of where the company is going, and to coach each employee to reach his or her potential, which, in turn, will help his company reach its potential.

"You have to paint the vision for your people. Most people see themselves not for what they are, but for less than what they are. People have lots of talents that they don't recognize or put to work because there's nobody there to push them or persuade them that they can do it. My employees have to borrow my vision to see farther than they themselves can see. One of my guys, for example, is going to make about $20,000 this month. When he first started here, he was really excited at the thought that he could make $4,000 a month. I told him 'You're a $10,000-plus guy.' He believed it. He bought into it. He believed what I told him, and that's very important. The key is to make your people better than you are. You have to see them for more than they are so they can see themselves for what they are. And then, when the guy gets to $4,000 a month, now he sees a little further. Now he can see to $6,000. When you get him to $6,000, now he can see to $8,000, and so on.

"Like the captain of a ship, you have to have a destination and you need to chart the course and sail. But everybody on that ship has a different task and different skills. Your job is to make sure that they do the best that they can do in their specific task. Let's take sales; not everyone sells the same way. It's my job to work with them one-on-one and teach them. 'This is what you're doing that's really great. This is what you can do better. Here's how we could do it better.'

"There are three things I look for in my salespeople: activity, first; productivity, second; and results, third. They have to move reasonably through all those three phases for me to believe that they're going to make it. In my industry, activity means making X number of calls. So, if I see they can make X number of calls, I know they can do the activity. If they don't make X number of calls, they can't do the activity and we either need to fix that or they need to go. Once I see the activity, I say, 'I know you can dial. Now do the right thing. Say the right thing.' That's productivity. 'How many presentations did you make? How many times did you try to close that sale?' Once I see that they understand productivity and that they understand the ratio of activity and productivity, then I look for results. 'Let's get your ratio from 1 of 100 to 2 of 100, and so on.' Within a year's time, you could be making $60,000 to $100,000 a year—no problem. If you're extra bright, I'd say you could do it in four to six months."

Lessons Learned

Leaders have many roles in an organization, but one of the most important is to set the vision and mission and to clarify the goals and values of the company. Marx Acosta-Rubio understands the power of vision and goals.

"I really believe that you will succeed as long as you persevere. Don't give up. Never give up! Stay true to your goal, but understand that whatever your original vision is, you may need to find different ways to get there. There's something called the ultimate success formula: Know what you want, take massive action, have sensory acuity, and change your approach until you reach your goal. I have a vision of what I want my company to be, but things have changed over the last three years. We used to do one thing, and now we do a couple different things, but our vision is still the same."

In addition to having a vision for the company, he tries to help each employee reach his or her potential—and thereby enable his company to reach its potential. He works with and coaches his employees. By painting the vision of what each person can do, then coaching him or her to do it, Acosta-Rubio unlocks his employees' potential and helps them achieve far more than they themselves ever imagined.

In addition to knowing what a leader *does*, Marx Acosta-Rubio's mentor taught him what a leader *is*. "Character is the most important thing. There are twelve pillars to character: courage, integrity, honesty, perseverance, wisdom, responsibility, humor, flexibility, confidence, good health, achievement, and living well. I think it's very important for an individual to have all twelve pillars. And I've learned you can't be a real leader without them."

RIDING THE ROLLER COASTER

Factsheet

Name:	Mark Moses
Title:	CEO
Company:	Platinum Capital Group
Type of Business:	Financial Services
Location:	Irvine, California
Annual Revenue:	$40 million
Employees:	450
Years in Business:	Not disclosed
The Edge:	Turncoat employees and changing markets putting the company on the brink of filing Chapter 7 bankruptcy.

The Story

After he sold his first company, Student Painters, Mark Moses began looking for something new to do. It didn't really matter to Mark what it was; he just wanted to get back into business. He and a partner hooked up and started Platinum Capital Group. Soon, Mark and his partner were in the home improvement loan business, sending out about half a million mailers a month and making about $250,000 a month. But Moses was soon to experience the impact of turncoat employees, changing market conditions, huge personal exposure, and near personal bankruptcy.

≈ 39 ≈

"On October 17, 1996, my friend, best man in my wedding, a guy I had hired into my company, resigned, and told me he had gotten this big job going to work for a Wall Street firm and so on and so forth. But he was really setting up a competing company down the street and hiring away all our people. I quickly got a court injunction, a restraining order and all that stuff, but the damage had already been done and the pain was only beginning. Prior to his leaving we had committed to moving into a 25,000 square foot facility. And we were sending out 500,000 mailers a month—we had made quite a bit of an investment in our marketing program. The phones were starting to ring, but I had hardly anyone to answer them. On October 31 I fired everybody who was left and reinterviewed the entire staff to see whether they were true to me and loyal, and whether they were serious about helping us build the company. I was in my Halloween costume when I did it.

"We went down to 40 people and, ultimately—when it was all over—I ended up with only 20. With 20 people I moved into that 25,000 square foot facility because I had already committed to the lease. It was just ridiculous. Everyone thought I was crazy being in this 25,000 square foot space with only 20 people. Every year I do an annual 'State of the Company' address similar to the President of the United States doing a State of the Union address. And this particular year I needed our folks to think big. We had to think big, or we were dead. I hired an 8,000-pound elephant, and I rode it down the streets of Irvine. We had torn down a wall in our building, and I rode that elephant into our annual meeting. The message was that if we think big and act big, we *will* be big. I was trying to make a point to our employees. I didn't realize that we would be in every local newspaper—the front page of the *Los Angeles Times* and the *Orange County Register*—and that NBC would pick it up nationwide. It was nuts.

"We rebuilt our center and, within a year, we had 275 people there. We were sending out 5 million mailers a month and making about $1 million a month. We were number 10 on the Inc. 500. We were the number one fastest growing business in L.A. We won the Blue Chip Enterprise Award for overcoming adversity. I was a finalist for businessperson of the year. All that was really great stuff. Just think where we were a short time ago! Very exciting and very cool.

"In '97 and '98 we had two offers for the company, one for $30 million and one for $56 million. And we were willing to do each of those deals, but both of them fell through. And then in October of '98—October is not a good month for me—Wall Street decided they weren't going to securitize the loans that we were handling anymore—our bread and butter. We went from earning $1 million a month to losing $1 million a month, had a massive layoff, and we closed our Irvine center. It was the pits.

"So we spent the next month in a conference room with a white board and a flip chart, and we built an entire business plan for an entirely new business structure. But as were building our plan, we sucked through all our cash. We ran out of money. And closing down the center had left us with ongoing liabilities that we could not meet. As we were writing our plan we said 'What can we do? Should we file Chapter 11 and restructure?' But we knew if we filed Chapter 11, all of the work that we had done—all the branches that we had brought on board, all the mortgage brokers that had joined us—would ultimately end up leaving us. So we elected not to file Chapter 11 but to act like we were in it.

"We had borrowed as much as we could from family and friends. I personally had $350,000 in credit card debt that had been carrying payroll and carrying the company because I really believed in our vision. But on October 10 we realized we weren't going to make it. I went to the bankruptcy lawyers and said 'We're going to have to file Chapter 7.' And the day I was filling out the schedules, my partner went to an entrepreneurial meeting and happened to meet a guy who had just sold his business for $150 million cash. My partner said to him, 'Hey, we're in dire straits here. Would you consider looking at our business plan and maybe helping us out? We're tapped out and we're ready to file for bankruptcy, but we've got an awesome business plan, and we'll do anything to just stay in the game.' So as I'm filing out the bankruptcy schedules, he calls and tells me not to sign anything. He meets with this guy. The guy flies back to Montana and calls us the next day and says 'I've got 31 questions.' We said 'We'll answer all 31 questions!' We spent about two and a half hours on the phone with him and answered all his questions. He said 'I'll let you know tomorrow.' We were looking for $1 million because we knew that that could get us through.

"He came back the next day and said 'Well, I have three questions to ask you.' And all three questions were no-brainers. And he said 'If I give you half a million, do you think you can find the other half a million somewhere else?' We said, 'Oh, yes, sir. We can.' Within a couple of days, he wrote us a check for half a million dollars, and that gave us enough fuel in the engine to get us going. At the same time, I'd been talking to an old buddy of mine who had his own investment bank. And when the Montana guy stepped up and wrote the half-million-dollar check, my friend said he knew it was a good deal, and he elected to come in and raise another $1.5 million for us. In addition to that, we talked friends and family into converting about $1 million of current debt to equity in the company and ultimately ended up raising in total $3 million over a six-month period.

"Today we have 65 branches around the country. We grew our business in the past year from 23 offices to 65 and are planning on going to 170 by the end of 2002. We grew our revenues from $10 million to $32 million. We went from $500 million in loan volume to over a billion dollars this past year and we went from 200 employees that we had at the end of 2000 to 500 and are going to 1,500 this year. And we expect to end up at $2.5 billion in volume and about $80 million in revenue for the year 2002. That's where we're headed. We're very profitable again. We've built an incredible management team over the past year and it's been an unbelievable ride."

Lessons Learned

Attitude is one of the major determinants of whether you will get through financial hard times. Throughout all his financial ups and downs—and there were many—Mark Moses kept his positive atti-tude, sure that despite the setbacks he was experiencing, he would overcome them and ultimately succeed. And that's exactly what he did. Did he make mistakes? Sure he did. He had built a com-pany that derived almost all of its revenue from a particular kind of loan instrument. When Wall Street dropped support for these loans, Moses was left without anything to sell. Diversifying his product offerings—as he has done in his current business—could have prevented much of the pain that he, his investors, and his employ-ees went through.

But, says Moses, "When my buddy left and took so many of my employees, that almost sent us to the edge. It was major adversity. I could have shut down my business and walked away because it was virtually done anyway. When we ran out of money or when the market collapsed in '98, I could have run away from that, too. But each time this adversity allowed me to build something new and better than I had before. You've got to hunker down and get in, work hard, build your new vision, and reinvent yourself. And if you do that, there's a rainbow at the end of the deal. Everybody who knows me has heard me say that a million times. I've said it through every crisis we've had and the core group of people that have stayed with us through those times have heard me say it over and over. I really believe it.

"One of my other lessons is to learn how to plan. Figure out where you want to be a year from now or two years from now or five years from now and work backward to get there. For example, let's say I want to do $100 million in revenue. I'll work the plan backward from my goal of $100 million in revenue: I need to have this many branches, I need to have this many people, I need my margins to be X. You build the whole thing backward.

"Finally, I always try to raise more capital than I need because you never know what's going to happen that will require more money. And I never worry about dilution of equity. I figure I'd rather own 10 percent of something great, than 100 percent of the lemonade stand in front of my mom's house!"

PAY ME NOW OR PAY ME LATER

Factsheet

Name:	Joshua Schecter
Title:	Managing Partner
Company:	ONLINE Business Services, Inc.
Type of Business:	Payroll services
Location:	San Antonio, Texas
Annual Revenue:	$1.1 million
Employees:	13
Years in Business:	Company founded March 1993
The Edge:	Employee problems jeopardizing client relationships; accountability declining as the company grew.

The Story

Joshua Schecter and his brother Jeff started a payroll business, ONLINE Business Services, Inc. in San Antonio, Texas, even though neither knew anything about payroll or accounting. Joshua was a computer consultant, and Jeff was a manager for a local Nissan car dealership. They decided that doing someone's payroll every two weeks, and getting paid for it each time, would be a great business opportunity. And right they were. But in order to create this great opportunity, the brothers realized they needed talented employees to help them build the business. But when employee problems jeopardized client relationships, and the business itself, the Schecter brothers realized they needed to make some changes.

According to Schecter, "We started doing time and attendance, and that quickly led to doing payroll. The software that we were using was terrible. We learned pretty quickly that we needed to know a lot about payroll—whether we wanted to or not—because we had an obligation to our customers. So we started getting pretty good at it. After a while, we had an opportunity to license a product that opened up the 50- to 2,000-employee market for us, and we've just been going gangbusters since then.

"In our business, that human element is the one thing that really makes a difference—and it can be a tremendous challenge. When you're an entrepreneur, you're a plate spinner. You try to keep all kinds of different things up in the air, and run from plate to plate to make sure they don't all come crashing to the ground. But you reach a point where you can't spin any more plates and you have to turn over some of the plates to people who, hopefully, you trust. And we've found that they also need to be people that share the same vision and values, and they're not easy to find.

"We've had managers, for example, who really caused us a lot of problems. We make tax deposits for our clients. Well, guess what? Ten years ago when I was doing it, that sucker was paid on every due date because there's a penalty if it's not. But when you turn that duty over to somebody else, they don't always have the same commitment to get it done, don't care about or understand the ramifications of not doing it right. They'll say, 'Well, it's getting late. I'll just leave it until tomorrow morning.' But the IRS doesn't buy that—or other things, like skipping a calendar date on somebody's payroll. When we're processing a payroll, skipping a date really affects our deposit schedule and when it picks up next time, we have to pay late penalties.

"The number one challenge in a growing business is transferring your spirit—that entrepreneurial spirit that enables you to get it all done, get it done right, and go above and beyond the requirements. We try to do that through empowerment, incentives, and paying people well. But that still doesn't guarantee success. For a while we had a very high turnover rate while we were trying to find people who share our values. Our values include things like honesty, integrity, doing your job with a smile, doing it right the first time. We may hire people we think are on the same page with us, but sometimes they turn out to be very good actors or actresses. We've got a crew now that we think is all on the same page with us.

"We use the football analogy. We like to think of our business as a football game. The playing field is the marketplace. One sideline is our set of values. The other sideline is our financial wherewithal. You can step out of bounds on either of those. The end zone is the goal. And what we're trying to do is get to the goal line, and have a good time while we're satisfying all of our values, staying within budget, and pleasing our customers. We're on about the five-yard line right now; we're about to score. Our operations people meet every day, and once a week we meet company-wide, and we talk about our values at each of these meetings.

"In our business, there are known milestones where you have to reengineer what you do. There's one at 400 clients, and there's another at 1,000 clients; we're just going through the first one right now. Every time we hit a milestone we have to reinvent the business. What works when you're one size doesn't work for the next size. I remember when I could call all my clients in one afternoon. Now it would take me three days just to dial all the numbers.

"And when we have to reinvent the business, there are always some people who fight the new system and will not make it. For example, we have empowered employees to cross-train other employees in different aspects of their jobs. We asked someone to train new employees about a particular facet of his job. He said, 'Sure, no problem,' but he never actually trained them. We found out through the grapevine—it's not something he admitted to—that he felt like he owned the keys to his job. I guess he thought that by training someone else to do his job he was reducing his own value. But in our company, it's the complete opposite. He would have become more valuable. I figure you have to be a team player, and if you're not, then you can't stay here and be on our team. That's just the way it is. We've faced a similar challenge with a few other employees. We try to work with them, but if we can't work it out, we have to fire them."

Lessons Learned

The payroll business is fast-paced and there is no room for errors. No one wants to have to tell their employees, "Sorry, you won't be receiving your paychecks this week; we had some technical difficulties." When clients hire ONLINE Business Services, they do so because they know they will get terrific customer service, that all deadlines will be met, and that payroll will work like a finely tuned clock. Ensuring that this will be the case, while dealing with a large staff, doesn't "just happen." It takes the ongoing attention of the company's leaders and talented and dedicated employees who share the same vision and values that they do.

Says Schecter, "I think entrepreneurs want to do everything themselves. They've always done it that way. They're good at spinning plates—up to a point. But we've learned our lesson. We're more than happy to let our talented employees help us keep those plates spinning and keep even more of them up in the air."

Joe Lynch is another entrepreneur with experiences similar to Joshua Schecter. Lynch, founder of Reachout Home Care, a medical staffing company that provides in-home care, has found that values are a key to the success of his company as well. But he has also put in a personnel system that helps weed out employees who don't fit and reinforces the fact that values matter in his company. "Values are everything to me. I wrote them down in a personnel handbook, which is handed to every single employee who walks in the door of this company. New employees go through an orientation, and we go over pages one and two of the handbook very carefully, and then they are handed their copy of the book. I don't care if they read every word or throw it in the trash. They are subject to the rules in that book as long as they work in my company.

"I have about 100 employees right now, and every day I have at least one personnel crisis. You have to deal with each crisis. It doesn't matter if the person is your best friend or worked for you for 10 years; if there's a problem, you have to write it up and put it on their personnel files. People don't like that, but you have to face the fact that sometimes people just don't work out in your company. And sometimes things go wrong between people. That doesn't mean people are bad. It just means that you need to make the case for why they need to change their behavior or leave your company. In other words, you need to cross your "t's" and dot your "i's" when it comes to personnel or it can come back to bite you. We have a "Three strikes you're out" policy. If a customer or fellow employee gets upset because an employee doesn't treat him or her properly, we write that up and put it in the employee's files. If that happens two more times, the employee is subject to termination. If an employee is caught smoking marijuana, doing drugs, or stealing, that's cause for instant termination."

Joshua Schecter and Joe Lynch understand that one of the leader's responsibilities is to select people who share their values and then hold them accountable. They make clear their expectations during the interviews, during orientation, in the employee handbook, and during discussions with employees. And when employees don't perform in accordance with the values, they let them know, write up the issue, and put it in their personnel files. They try to help them improve their performance, but they are also willing to fire them if the problems persist.

BACK TO WHERE IT ALL BEGAN

Factsheet

Name:	Bob Kirstiuk
Title:	President and CEO
Company:	Advantage Data Systems Corporation
Type of Business:	Wholesale aftermarket automobile parts
Location:	Vancouver, British Columbia
Annual Revenue:	$9 million
Employees:	110
Years in Business:	Company founded 1988
The Edge:	Successful company acquired by a dot-com, erasing ten years of equity and almost $50 million in capital.

The Story

When Bob Kirstiuk and a partner founded Advantage Data Systems Corporation in 1988, the idea was to help new car dealerships maximize their profit opportunity in their wholesale parts business. The company grew quickly, expanding into Alberta, Ontario, and Quebec, then the United States, and then England.

Says Kirstiuk, "We bootstrapped our start-up the whole way. At times, when we didn't have enough money to pay salaries, my partner and I were working for the company with no compensation. Many times in the life of our business, we had 10 or 20 credit cards maxed out—typical bootstrapping. In 1993 we ventured south of the border, opening operations in Seattle and Detroit. In 1994 we were contacted by some folks in England about expanding our business there, so we entered into a joint venture with a business in the UK. Today, we have operations coast to coast in Canada, the United States, and the UK as well.

"I was looking to raise capital because we wanted to expand the business. And we were looking at this whole dot-com phenomenon and thought we could leverage our business and get into the dot-com gold rush. A friend of mine mentioned that he heard about a business—Carstation.com—that had recently raised some significant capital. He suggested we get together and talk. Long story short, within a week we had a letter of intent for Carstation.com to buy our business. We sold the business to them, and part of that deal was for my partner and me to stay with the new company because a substantial amount of the compensation we received was in the form of stock options.

"I relocated to San Francisco. Based on the acquisition, we went out and closed on a second round of funding, around $35 million. We had real revenues coming in, so that served to substantiate the business model. The objective was to get the company to an IPO in the year 2000, but when the market started to crash around April of that year, we realized that it was going to be a longer road than we anticipated. Within a few months we realized that it was not going to happen at all.

"By that time, we had built quite a large infrastructure here in San Francisco. We had about 250 employees, and a substantial burn rate. We had wanted to be the 800-pound gorilla in this automotive space. We had done everything right. We had hired people with a lot of experience and industry knowledge for the top team. We were getting good media feedback and *Forbes* and industry analysts were writing about Carstation.com as the real player in the space. Everything had come together really well. But when the market started to crash, things began to happen that were out of our control. It became very apparent, very quickly, that although we had raised a lot of capital—in the neighborhood of $50 million altogether—that wouldn't be enough for a long-term business. And our $5 million run rate couldn't support a company with 250 employees.

"We decided that we needed to reinvent ourselves. We needed to change the name of the company and get out of the dot-com arena. So we changed the company to OnStation Corporation. Toward the end of the year, we decided to spin off the Carstation.com part of the business, and we sold the Internet exchange to a joint venture created by three large companies that came into our space as a competitive response to what we were doing. We tried to partner with them, and they said, 'Sure we'll partner with you, but we want half of the company.' It was a very difficult time, and revenues in many of our markets were cannibalized by about 50 percent.

"After we sold the exchange software, the next question was what we were going to do with the rest of the organization, about 120 employees. I made a proposal to the board of directors: my partner and I would take back the business and assume the operating liability for the company. Shutting down the company and paying severance to more than 100 people, getting out of leases and such, would be an expensive option for them to pursue. And selling it to an outside party would have taken too much time.

"So on April 13, we closed the deal and reacquired our business—burn rate and all. We quickly restructured the business, taking it down to about 80 employees. The majority of those people are the people who were with us when we sold the business to Carstation.com. We were able to negotiate some funding from OnStation to get us through the first six months of operations. We're executing on our business plan, and the good news is that everybody in the company has performed way beyond our expectations. We turned the business around 180 degrees in the last six months. We're looking forward to going into the new year with some very aggressive expansion plans."

Lessons Learned

The dot-com phenomenon was an experience unlike any other that most entrepreneurs have experienced. Investors clamoring to be a part of the "next big thing"—whatever that next big thing might be—pumped billions of dollars into companies and they quickly expanded. But when the bubble burst, many of these companies with high burn rates could not restructure themselves quickly enough and went down in flames. They became virtually worthless almost overnight. Kirstiuk had two opportunities to cash out his stake in his business—to take the money and run—but he chose not to.

Says Kirstiuk, "Looking back on our dot-com venture, I think the one thing that just amazes me is that we raised and spent so much money. Even today, it is hard to comprehend how we were able to spend that much money so quickly. Today, we're back to bootstrapping the business. The company—and we—are much more mature than a couple of years ago. We learned a tremendous amount through our dot-com venture. There are no regrets, and everybody feels that they grew a lot during that experience. I talk with my partner about that all the time. But you know, even if we only had $3 million in the bank, that's all we'd need to grow our company from a $6 million to a $50 million business. That was a real lesson learned.

"I learned something else. Everyone began thinking this was going to be our opportunity to get rich quick. We were going to do an IPO, and we were all going to become millionaires. When you give out stock options, you hope that makes everybody feel like an owner of the business. I thought I would come into the office on the weekend, and there would be 50 people there working all hours of the day and night. I was shocked when that didn't happen. There were too many nine-to-fivers. I guess they really didn't know what they were supposed to be doing, or maybe they did not know how what they did affected the overall objective of the organization.

"I think there are some very basic principles that apply to any real business that people who have bootstrapped have learned.

One of the reasons we have been successful is because we have alignment within our organization, and that only happens through very regular communication that cascades down throughout the entire organization. Otherwise, you end up with a lot of disconnects, and people don't really know what they're supposed to be doing.

"We have daily huddles within our entire organization at every level, starting with the executive team. I have a call with my executive team every morning at 8:30 A.M., from my managing director in Europe to my sales director in New York to our operating directors in Vancouver. The call is 15 to 30 minutes long each day. And my sales manager has a call with his management team, as do all the other managers. And every day at 11:30 A.M. our office gets together for a 5- to 10-minute meeting. Once a week we have a bigger meeting that lasts half an hour, and we go through what happened last week and what's going to happen next week. This helps us get alignment between all the functional units: sales, marketing, finance, and IT. It also enables us to get feedback from our customer base through the sales organization, to the whole organization so that the marketing group or IT group does not develop new projects or new programs that are not aligned to the needs of our customers.

"We establish our top five priorities for the company for each year, and the top five for each quarter, then we identify the number one goal that we want to achieve. We publish that. We also publish our critical numbers. We want everybody to know what those numbers are. We focus on three numbers: (1) incremental revenue growth; (2) number of customer contacts we make daily; and (3) new client prospect presentations, which give us information about our pipeline of new business opportunities. We post those numbers on our intranet site every day and refer to those numbers during our daily huddles and weekly meetings.

"You know, my partner and I could be out of this company by now—living the good life. When we negotiated the original deal with CarStation.com, they agreed that if they ever divested our company, there would be a payout to my partner and me. So when

OnStation was considering closing down our (former) company, it would have been a better financial decision for us personally to have agreed to shut it down and walk away.

"But we offered to repurchase it—burn rate and all—because we felt a commitment to the people who had worked for us over the years. A lot of those people had been with us five or ten years. They had mortgages and families and a love of what they do. So we decided that the right thing to do was to get the company back, make it healthy again, and create long-term career opportunities for those people who supported us. And we're doing that."

LOSING A PARTNER

Factsheet

Name:	Charles Tetrick
Title:	President & CEO
Company:	Walz Tetrick Advertising
Type of Business:	Advertising agency
Location:	Shawnee Mission, Kansas
Annual Revenue:	$8 million
Employees:	20
Years in Business:	Company founded 1990
The Edge:	Partner dying suddenly without a shareholder agreement or contingency plan.

The Story

Soon after graduating from the University of Kansas, Charles Tetrick started his own small advertising agency and ran it for three years before he met John Walz, an older man who had a well-established advertising agency in the Kansas City area. Walz was looking for a way to slow down and play a little more golf. Since Tetrick was looking for a way to take a big jump with his own client base, it seemed like a match made in heaven.

"In 1993, we put our two firms together and changed the name to Walz Tetrick Advertising. But eighteen months later, John had a heart attack and died—with no will. He was 59, and I never expected him to die. I was only 26 at the time, and it hit me like a truck. It was a big shock to the business as well.

"We had a client base that had been around for quite some time. Tension Envelope is a client that's been with us for 34 years—since the day John started the company. We worked with Harmon Industries, which was later bought out by GE. But we had a small shop of five or six people at the time of his death.

"When John died, I had never even met these key clients. They were his clients, and he played it close to the vest. I wasn't sure if they were going to stick with the firm since they didn't even know me. I pictured myself going to them, knocking on their door and saying, 'John's gone; are you going to stick with us?' and them looking at me, thinking 'Who is this kid?' Fortunately, most of our clients decided to give us a chance.

"When he died, there was a lot of ambiguity about the company's ownership. He had by far the majority of the equity—the split was like 95/5 or 90/10 or something like that. I had a really small stake in the big picture. Of course, after John died, his estate was very curious about the value of the firm. There's always a lot of ambiguity about what a company like ours is worth because it is privately held, and it's a service business. There isn't much you could liquidate and sell off and come up with a number. So we had a real challenge in trying to structure a deal that worked for his estate, that made sense for the company, and that made sense for me. It took us 60 to 90 days to get things settled with the estate, come up with a game plan, and determine where we were going to go with the company. The following days—even years—were filled with the challenges of buying the business from my partner's estate—complete with wife, ex-wife, kids, stepkids—and no will.

"After he died, we convened everyone in the conference room, and I told everybody, 'We're going to have to find a way to make a go of this and we're going to have to make the targets.' We had a four-year plan that was written just before John died, and we tied what we did with his estate to the plan. We put a deal together based on a four-year buyout. We agreed that if the accounts stuck around, then we would pay the estate a percentage of their proceeds, but if clients left us, then we wouldn't pay the estate for them. We had a lot of John's family at the table, along with their attorneys. It was an emotional issue for everybody.

"The four-year plan became the focus of everything we did. Year one of this plan was 'Don't make a ripple in the water.' It was completely client focused—making sure that they didn't see the real trauma that was going on behind the scenes. Make sure the clients are taken care of and above all just keep it going. Years two and three of the plan were 'Real internal focus.' I wanted to make sure the salaries were right, which they hadn't been for a lot of the staff. We invested heavily in equipment and technology to make sure we were up to speed. We physically moved our offices because we wanted to shake off some of the old images and the old ways of doing business. The fourth year was 'All about growth.' I hired another senior account supervisor who was a really big hitter. He had had a stint with General Mills working on marketing programs for Bacos, Wheaties, and Betty Crocker and spent about eight years as an account supervisor with another big agency. He really brought some of the senior expertise back to us.

"Starting with the fourth year of our plan—which was also the last year of the buyout—we had our current clients under control. We had all the internal operations in pretty good shape. Frankly they were much better than they'd ever been. And then we tried to concentrate on how we could grow the company to a different place. We're up to 20 people today—from five employees when my partner died. This year our capitalized billing should be in the $6 million to $8 million range. We're in line to be probably ten-ish. When John died we were in the $1.5 million to $2 million range."

Lessons Learned

When entering into a business partnership, few of us consider what would happen to the business if one of the partners dies unexpectedly. When his partner died only a year and a half after they teamed up, Tetrick suddenly found himself struggling to keep the business running, dealing with his partner's family, and negotiating a plan to buy the business from the estate.

A shareholder agreement is essential. It should have an exit provision that specifies the terms and conditions under which a partner can leave, legal provisions that spell out what partners can or cannot do after they leave, and provisions about happens if a partner dies. Fortunately for Tetrick, the family was willing to let him buy the business. They might have kept it and tried to run it themselves, sold it to another firm, or closed it down. If you don't have a shotgun buy-out provision that specifies the terms and conditions under which the remaining partner(s) can buy the business from the estate, you may suddenly find you're de facto partners with the spouse or the children of your now-deceased partner.

Says Charles Tetrick, "I learned the importance of good communication. We made sure everybody in the firm knew where everything stood. 'Here's what we're going to try to do with the business. Here are the problems I see in our way. Here's how I see growth of new business coming to us, and here's who I think can do it.' We have stated goals, too. We let everyone know what we're shooting for and how as a team we're going to get there. We set a revenue goal, and each supervisor is responsible for managing anything from half a million to a million dollars' worth of business.

"I also learned a lot about the importance of culture and hiring people that fit the culture. We put an enormous premium on our culture and our environment here. When we hire a new supervisor, we may spend eight months on it to make sure we get the right people and make sure it's going to work. In the first four years when I was paying off John's estate, we simply could not make any mistakes. They were getting 8 percent of the revenue, and at the end of the day there was not a whole lot left. We had to make sure we were making the right moves and hiring the right people.

"I do a lot of due diligence and when checking references, I go well beyond the list they give us. I'll call some folks from other offices to get a feel for the candidates. We've hired a couple of people this year, and I haven't even looked at their resumes. They've been screened by the appropriate department, so I don't worry about their credentials. I spend some time with them and try to get to know them as people. If you can ferret out the real key issues of honesty, ethics, and morals, then the odds are you're not going to get burned too badly when you hire someone."

INHERITING PROBLEMS

Factsheet

Name:	Anne Bain
Title:	President & CEO
Company:	Amrel-Byrnes Company
Type of Business:	Heavy and highway construction
Location:	Cincinnati
Annual Revenue:	$18 million
Employees:	Seasonal; about 100
Years in Business:	Fifth generation company
The Edge:	Father dying suddenly; daughter having to quickly learn the business and run it; clashed with partner about an unclear partnership agreement.

The Story

Anne Bain was in medical school, expecting her first child, when her father was killed in a car accident in 1992. The year he died, the company lost a lot of money, and she had to decide whether to stay in medical school and leave the settlement to the lawyers, or leave medical school and come home to run the business. She chose the business.

"The first year a multitude of things went wrong. A customer who was 95 percent of the sales of a sister company stopped letting work for the first six months. In July we had 28 days of rain, we had a developer who stiffed us for more than $1 million, and we lost $2.6 million on sales of less than $20 million. Nobody would tell me anything, and then suddenly people started calling me and telling me the company didn't have any credit, it hadn't paid people in months, and the employees didn't like the guy running it who was my father's partner. I took the next six months and went through the check runs, learned who our vendors were, learned what we bought from them and what we did with it, and negotiated with the five biggest vendors that we hadn't paid off. I took old invoices, converted them to notes, and paid them out over the remainder of the year.

"We had a highly competent management team in place, with the exception of Joe, the partner my dad had brought in. I felt very supported by the team, but I spent a lot of time fighting with Joe. Although he owned only a third of the company, Joe had a buy-sell agreement that spelled out his right to be an employee, his right to be president, and his right to a certain salary. The contract said that if my dad was to die while Joe only owned one-third of the stock, then Joe was to immediately purchase the next one-third. Well, Joe's lawyer's definition of "immediately" was three to four years down the line—which wasn't exactly our definition. Joe didn't want to leave because he had no place else to go. I didn't want to leave because the moment I did, I was sure there wouldn't be a company left. After a year of fighting Joe, I finally bought him out.

"I credit my success to four things. My father was very respected, and people operated on the assumption that the apple doesn't fall far from the tree. Second, Joe was not well liked or trusted, so almost anyone would have been better received than he was. Third, I didn't know anything about the business or about construction. I was very honest about that, I asked a lot of questions, and I let people teach me. I never made any bones about the fact that I didn't know things. Somebody later said to me, 'The smartest thing you ever did was to let people teach you.' Finally, I realized that 'she's her father's daughter.' and 'thank God she's not Joe,' could carry me to a certain point, but then I had to prove myself. So I became good at the numbers and the management end of things."

Lessons Learned

Anne Bain inherited a host of problems from her father. Her story is a good illustration of what happens when you pick the wrong person as partner: if you should die unexpectedly, your partner is left to manage the company, your major asset. "My dad offered Joe one-third of the company when he bought in, one-third in five years, and one-third in seven years. The idea was to bring in a guy who had some experience in the industry but was young enough to be trained. My father got to retain the title of chairman of the board and maintain ownership for the first five years, so it was a way for him to have his cake and eat it too. Unfortunately, my dad really wanted to retire, so he didn't spend a lot of time training Joe, and then he died."

When the company began losing money, Bain was sure Joe would never be able to pull the company back from the edge, so she fought to get the company back. This story illustrates one more reason you need to be careful about the person you pick as a partner. Ask yourself this question: If I die, will the person I pick as partner (or the person who is now my partner) be able to lead and manage the company so as to fulfill the terms and conditions of the shareholder agreement? Or will he or she drive the company into extinction and rob my family of its inheritance?

Although Anne Bain's story deals with partnership issues, it also deals with leadership issues. The edge is rarely so black and white that only one issue threatens your business. Bain was not afraid to have people working for her who knew more about the business than she did. She inherited a highly competent management team, asked good questions, and let people do their job. She also let her people teach her. She identified critical performance indicators, tracked them carefully, and managed resources. Bain also had the courage to get rid of someone who wasn't performing as expected. All of these are major responsibilities of a leader of a growth company.

BUILDING A BUSINESS OR
BUILDING A COMPANY

Factsheet

Name:	Kevin Daum
Title:	CEO
Company:	Build Your Dream Home
Type of Business:	Financial services
Location:	Alameda, California
Annual Revenue:	$1 million
Employees:	9
Years in Business:	Company founded 2000
The Edge:	Started a second company, lost a lot of money, came close to losing the first company.

The Story

Kevin Daum already had a successful company—Stratford Financial—when he decided to found a second one. "Thanksgiving of 2000, we founded a new company called Build Your Dream Home (BYDH). We raised $2 million for BYDH inside of four months. We put that all on an angel basis at a $5 million money valuation. We really did well. We didn't create a product; we created a company. We were all ready for venture capital when the market shifted, and it soon became clear the company wasn't going to get venture capital funding.

"In the meantime, Stratford held its ground. However, once the cash flow was in place, my old partner basically abandoned it, and morale was pretty bad. Fortunately, the business was strong, the business was repetitive, and the loyalty of some key members was so great that the company survived, almost on its own.

"Since we probably weren't going to get venture capital funding for BYDH, the question was whether we should merge it with Stratford. I had a talk with my partner: 'It's pretty clear you don't want to be a part of this. You've got all this debt hanging on you with the company. You don't need it. Why don't you just walk away?' And he did.

"So I had my first company back for what it was: basically breaking even, paying me nothing, and about three-quarters of a million dollars in debt. Fortunately, two-thirds of that was private debt, not bank debt. BYDH moved in and immediately Stratford got a little shot in the arm: people, equipment, activities, things going on. However, we made the decision that if we did not find a company for BYDH to merge with by mid-November, we would close it by the end of the year and return some money to the investors rather than go bankrupt. There wasn't a whole lot of money to return—only about a penny and a half on the dollar—but we would give them the tax deduction before the end of the year. And that's exactly what happened.

"We were able to reduce Stratford's debt a little more, and even had a little money in the bank to get us through the winter when we started the new year. I had a team of people who were incredibly loyal to the company but were really pissed at me. They felt that I had gone off to do a lot of fun stuff with BYDH and left them at Stratford Financial.

"So I decided to go to Europe. I said, 'You guys keep this thing running. As long as it's profitable and as long as we can continue to reduce our debt, I'm a happy guy.' Near the end of the first quarter it became clear they weren't making it. They said, 'Okay, we're ready for you to come back now.' And slowly but surely, over the second quarter, I rebuilt the morale. But we still weren't making it, and in the middle of the second quarter we pretty much hit bottom. It all just finally came to the end. The company just wasn't there, and the plan just wasn't there. And there was no energy driving it.

"So I called all our creditors and said, 'We have a choice. We can blow this thing up today, or we can put a new plan in place that gives this company a chance. I'm not paying you for 90 days. And that's your best shot at getting your money back.' And they agreed.

"We developed a new plan. And the good news is that we have turned around our production. The pipeline was down to about $18 million in loans in our system. I'm sitting here with over $32 million today. I've trimmed the overhead down to $35,000 a month and that includes debt reduction and a salary for me. We're still struggling with cash flow, but that should soon resolve itself. Our debt has been reduced to about $650,000. The phones are starting to ring. We've got new plans in place, and we're capitalizing on what our core business has been all along—the construction line. At long last, we have a future."

Lessons Learned

Entrepreneurs love to create new ventures. There's excitement in the act of creating new enterprises that is both intoxicating and incredibly satisfying. Often, this drive to create—and the optimism or belief that they can do it all—leads entrepreneurs to take on more than they can handle.

Kevin Daum learned that he couldn't do it all. It took him a while to realize that in order to build a company you have to understand the upside and downside of growth. You have to learn to capitalize on your personal strengths and compensate for your weaknesses. And you have to understand the difference between building a business and building a company.

Daum notes, "I've learned a hell of a lot about humility. One big lesson I have learned is how much more important it is to identify what I don't know than what I do know. I'm the grandkid of an entrepreneur and child of a would-be entrepreneur. I didn't know that growth could be bad. I so wanted to be on the Inc. 500 list. I'd fallen in love with it and didn't understand there was a downside to that. I didn't understand the importance of the bottom line. I was a sales guy. I thought I could sell my way out of anything."

Daum also learned the difference between building a business and building a company. "With a business, you may make money, but if you take a vacation or decide not to be there anymore, the business falls away. Many companies are just a business. A successful company has several businesses. A successful company has a structure, a set of values, a culture, an organization, its own self-sustaining means for hiring, firing, and weeding out people, improving systems, creating new ideas, creating new businesses, and that's what has value. You need to make a conscious choice whether to build a business or a company."

To build a strong, growth-oriented company, a good idea is just the beginning. A leader needs to create a clear mission, create a culture to support the mission, build a solid infrastructure, and hire the right people. Failure to address any of those factors could not only mean failure to grow, but it could also prevent the creation of any value in the company.

"Many entrepreneurs build a business and get it to the point where Stratford Financial was —where it's growing, it's rocking, it's a lot to manage, and it's all about maintenance. And if they haven't put the systems in place, haven't put the culture in place, and it's not a living, breathing, self-sustaining organism, they don't like it anymore. So they go out and try to sell it, but they find that nobody is interested in buying it. All they are interested in is buying *them*. And they wonder, 'What do I have to do to sell my company?' I've finally learned the answer to that question.

"I'm now spending energy putting a culture together, putting systems in place, and it's incredibly frustrating and hard. It does not happen as fast as I would like it to. And it takes time away from transacting business. So there's a cost in the short term, and I do understand that there are factors I can't control. But in three years I am hoping this company will be profitable, that it will have a positive margin that is measurable by all involved, and that it will have value. I've learned that it's not worth anything to me if it's not worth anything to anybody else. And the difference between building a business and building a company is the most valuable lesson I've learned."

≈ Wrap-up ≈

As your company grows, you need to keep asking yourself, "What is it that only I can do?" The answer to that question will change, over time, depending on your company's stage of development. At certain stages of growth, it is critical that you learn to delegate so you can lead and manage the company to its next stage of growth. Joshua Schecter realized that he had to stop trying to keep all the plates spinning and began hand some off some of those plates to other people. Delegation is a very important lesson for every company owner to learn.

But there are some core responsibilities that the leader can never delegate and our stories illustrate what they are. For example, it's your job to define the mission of the company, to specify the values under which the company should operate, and to create the culture. Frank Nemiroff blames himself for the employee theft and timecard fraud—because he never took the time to define the mission and values of the organization. Now that he has, he's insisting that his employees live by the values and achieve performance expectations—and he's willing to fire them if they don't. Joe Lynch says that values are everything to him, and he's written them down in a handbook. He measures his employees' behavior against these values; three strikes and they're out. In order to build a company, rather than just a business, Kevin Daum has realized the importance of defining his mission and values, and building a company culture.

You need to communicate, all the time, in many different ways to your employees. Bob Kirstiuk believes that alignment within his company has enabled him to be successful, with less money, and that good communications has facilitated that alignment. A car with a well-tuned engine and balanced tires can travel farther on less gas. A company that is aligned is more efficient and effective—and needs less money to grow. It requires that you set goals, communicate, get people aligned, and execute on the goals. "Daily Huddles" are one of the hallmarks of Bob's company: Every day, every manager has a 15–30 minute conversation with his or her direct reports, wherever they are located. Every day, at 11:30 A.M. the people in his office have a short meeting, with a longer meeting once a week. This regular communication enables people closest to the customers to provide feedback, it prevents disconnects, it provides opportunities to clarify what people need to do, and it enables managers to report how well the company is achieving its goals. This has enabled Bob's company to grow and run much more efficiently—and effectively—without a lot of outside money. Charles Tetrick found that frank and open communication was essential when dealing with all the parties-at-interest to his partner's estate, and regular communication was essential for keeping his team aligned and executing on the plan.

It's all about the people. It's your job to hire people and build the team; if you have a good team, then let them execute and don't try to second-guess or micro-manage. Anne Bain took over her father's company after he died. She knew almost nothing about the business, yet she was able to succeed because she had a great top team. She recognized that almost everyone on that team knew more than she did—and she let them do their jobs without second guessing them. On the other hand, she got rid of someone who was not performing and was endangering the future of the company. She taught herself what the numbers mean and learned how to be a good manager. Doug Mellinger learned a similar lesson: find the best people for the job, train them, coach them, provide opportunities for them to grow, help them achieve their goals, but if they don't perform, then fire them. Marx Acosta-Rubio suggests that your job as leader is to make sure that you select the good people, create the right environment for them to succeed, believe in them, and make it possible for them to perform at their highest level.

You have to plan and stay focused, but there may be times when you will have to re-invent your company. Ken Wolf learned that lack of focus and distraction pushed his company to the edge. Although he didn't fail, he lost a whole lot of money. Mark Moses learned how to plan backwards. He suggests that you envision where you want to be in three years, then plan backwards and identify what you need to do to get there. On the other hand, you need to be aware of what's happening in the environment, how that will impact your plans, and be flexible enough to change—even re-invent the company if need be. Mark discovered that he had to go back to the white board several times and re-invent the company: after his partner took most of his staff and set up a competing company, when Wall Street decided to stop securitizing the loans that he was handling, and when he ran through all his cash. The big lesson is to plan, stay focused on the plan, measure progress against plan, communicate regularly with your employees, but be willing to shift gears and re-invent your company if circumstances change dramatically.

After providing our Top Ten Lessons in Leadership, we'll share some stories and lessons learned about leading and managing people in the next section.

Top Ten Lessons in Leadership

The stories you've just read describe what entrepreneurs and CEOs have learned about leading a growth company. Together these stories illustrate the tasks and responsibilities of the leader:

1. Create the vision and direction for your company. Share that vision freely with partners, employees, investors, friends, and family.

2. Create a culture that reflects your vision and hire people whose personal values fit yours.

3. Set clear goals and track your progress.

4. Hire the right people for the job. Look for people who are self-motivated, able to handle change and deal with crises, are customer focused, and have the capacity to grow and develop.

5. Make sure employees understand the goals; coach them, set personal goals, then hold them accountable. Reward them if they achieve or surpass the goals and fire them if they don't. Get smarter about how to attract and retain great people.

6. Identify your goals, recognize where your business model is vulnerable, then develop a plan and execute it. Stay focused

and don't allow employees, yourself, or your partners to get distracted.

7. Be frugal with resources and make sure your expenditures add value to the company. Don't spend money just to satisfy your personal ego.

8. Take risks but balance them with possible outcomes. Don't bet the farm on one venture.

9. Be a leader in words and deeds.

10. Lead the company through the transitions of growth. Recognize that you will need to change your roles and responsibilities as the company grows. If you aren't able to lead the company through growth, then you need to be willing to step aside and find someone else who can.

SECTION 2

≈ People ≈

Section-at-a-Glance

Overview

Individual Profiles

Profile: Sam Boyer
The Edge: Choosing the right people and keeping them focused during the chaos of high growth.

Profile: Craig Pollard
The Edge: Transforming into a leader and manager during explosive growth.

Profile: Damon Gersh
The Edge: Overnight expansion of business by 50 times the original number of staff and subcontractors to help New York recover after September 11.

Profile: Howard Getson
The Edge: No accountability, inexperienced management causing huge opportunity costs and struggle to survive.

Profile: Alex Rusch
The Edge: Rapid hiring resulting in high declines in efficiency and customer service. Lack of processes and protocols caused poor performance.

Profile: Paul Hickey
The Edge: Hiring the wrong candidate for president three times in a row, resulting in new problems each time.

Wrap-Up

Top Ten Lessons in People

≈ People ≈
Overview

We entrepreneurs love the process of creating and selling. Some call it "the chase." We love to develop new markets, create new products or services, and sell to new customers. For a variety of reasons many of us don't focus enough time and attention on building an organization that can support the stresses and strains of growth. One of the most important aspects of building an organization is learning how to attract and retain great people and helping them achieve high performance. The stories in this section make it clear: if we want to grow, we've got to learn to manage people.

First we have to learn to select and hire the right people. In the last section we read several stories and lessons that illustrate you need to have a clear mission and vision—clear enough to explain to other people. The next step is to find people who can relate to your mission, are a good fit with your values and have the capacity to perform. Once you've found them, then you need to lead and manage them: share your vision with them, include them in the planning process, communicate regularly with them, measure achievement of the company's goals and their performance against goals, provide feedback, coach and train them, and be willing to fire anyone who does not operate according to your values or perform at the level expected.

As entrepreneurs we tend to be optimists, to assume that others think like we do. Sometimes we trust people more than we should.

We are also in a hurry—to reach a goal, to prove we can do something, to hit the window of opportunity. We are externally focused and assume that the internal stuff, the organizational stuff, will somehow take care of itself. But it doesn't. Only after we've been blindsided by a dishonest partner or disloyal employee do we realize that we need to pay more attention to building the organization and managing people. This book is full of stories of entrepreneurs who found themselves near the edge because they did not understand their responsibility to build the organization and manage people.

Management is different from leadership. Management is all about creating systems and standardizing processes, putting in checks and balances, and building an organization that can function without your doing every task yourself. Few entrepreneurs enjoy the tasks of managing. But after nearly losing the company—and having their faith in others severely shaken—most realize the importance of leading and managing people.

Sam Boyer had to learn how to select people who could handle the kind of change inherent in rapid growth, and it was a challenge to find them. He needed employees who would not be stressed by the fact that that he was reworking and changing methods and procedures every day. He searched for people who could keep performing when everything around them was in constant flux. You'll be surprised at what he looked for when he was interviewing candidates.

Craig Pollard has learned a lot about people. He's learned to hire people different from himself, and shares some tips on managing different kinds of people. He places a high premium on people who share his values and achieve their goals. Be sure to check out what he says about motivating people.

Paul Hickey made three bad hires for president before he got it right—with the help of a recruiter. He's learned a lot of lessons about what to look for when you're hiring someone, how to match them with the skills and capabilities needed to take the company to the next level, and he shares some valuable lessons about how to delegate and manage a successful transition.

Howard Getson now understands that not having the right people in the right positions crippled his company. The people in key positions were always one click behind what was needed to take the company to the next stage, but he didn't recognize that soon enough. When he finally realized what was happening, he didn't make changes as quickly as he should have. Next time he knows exactly what he'll do.

Alex Rusch advises fellow entrepreneurs to take more time when wording ads and interviewing people. He's also learned that people need systems and policies to guide their efforts, goals, and measures to track their productivity. Finally, he's learned not to wait too long and "hope" for improvement.

Damon Gersh figured out how to scale and grow rapidly in a very short period of time: do advance planning, develop guidelines, have a great team in place, get sub-contractors who are committed to you, trust people and hold them accountable. That enabled him to expand fifty times his normal size in two weeks in order to tackle a huge project: cleaning up New York City after the September 11 disaster.

You'll find these stories amazing and thought provoking. As you read them, think about the following questions:

- How do they find and select their best people? How do your company's personnel systems compare to theirs?

- What guidelines did they provide to their employees? Do your employees know what you want them to do? Do you need to develop guidelines, standards or measures to help them perform at peak levels?

- What did they learn about delegating to new people, especially top team members? What changes do you need to make when you delegate?

- How did they measure performance? How do you measure performance in your company?

- How did they hold people accountable and what did they do when people were not performing?

If you don't want to manage people, don't know how, or don't think you are the best person for the job—then read on. Our entrepreneurs either learned to become much better managers of people and hired others to help them, or they watched their company go over the edge. Don't let that happen to you.

Individual Profiles

BREWING UP A PERFECT BUSINESS

Factsheet

Name:	Sam Boyer
Title:	Co-Founder
Company:	Brothers Coffee
Type of Business:	Gourmet coffee producers
Location:	Denver, Colorado
Annual Revenue:	$140 million
Employees:	900
Years in Business:	Not disclosed
The Edge:	Choosing the right people and keeping them focused during the chaos of high growth.

The Story

Dennis and Sam Boyer started Brothers Coffee as a small, local seller of coffee to other businesses through office coffee programs. When Sam Boyer was approached by a grocery store to create blends of different coffees to sell retail, Boyer said "Why not?" This simple beginning quickly led to tremendous growth and success for the Denver-based company that created a new industry category: flavored coffee.

According to Boyer, "Dennis and I started with a couple of employees. I would roast up the coffee at night and do an all-nighter once or twice a week, ship the coffee the next day, then go home, go to bed, come back and do it all over again. By 1992 we had about 900 employees and $140 million in annual sales.

"After we started the business, we grew about 10 to 12 percent per month for about five years. We got recognized by *Forbes* and a couple other magazines—several times—as one of the top-100 fastest growing small businesses in America.

"From the very start, the biggest challenge was to keep our employees and our team members focused on the end goal, which was to build a company that satisfied customer expectations. The second challenge was to get our employees to sign up for constant change and constant reworking of the procedures and methods by which we did everything. Change is not something most folks welcome, but growth is all about change.

"We had to find people who were flexible, because sometimes we were literally constructing new processes and systems on top of them as they did their work. On the other hand, we were very flexible and allowed our employees a lot of discretion about how to make their work schedules fit their family requirements. We did lots of things to accommodate employee schedules without batting an eye. It takes a lot of understanding and personal commitment from everyone involved to manage the kind of growth that we had.

"My biggest challenge was getting the right kinds of employees who could handle the changes inherent in growth. During an interview, I found myself checking out their adaptability, the number of jobs they had held in the past—more being better—and asking some very simple questions about how they dealt with change. You can train people for the technical skills you need, but you really need people to have the core strength in people management, customer management, and crisis management when they walk in the door. We dealt with customer crises and production problems all the time, so when I hired people, I was more interested in their adaptability and personality than I was their work skill history."

Lessons Learned

Says Boyer, "Our leadership, our commitment to our employees and to our customers, has always been rooted in our values of excellence, honesty, and integrity. This applied, regardless of whether you were the manager of the floor or the person who rolled down the bags and inspected them to make sure that the labels were perfectly straight. We would not ship out any bag if the labels were not perfect. People's perception about what's in the package is often based on what they see on the outside of the package. So if the label's not straight, they think that the product's not as good.

"If an employee came up to us and said 'I have this idea,' we'd say 'Great! Let's try it on the next shift. And if it works, you can share in the success of the idea.' We would just go with it. Sometimes we knew an idea wasn't the best idea, but we'd give it a try anyway as an honor to the people who were serving the customer through our production channels.

"If they were trying to get their GED we would pay their GED fees. We were very concerned about people moving up the channels of education because we wanted our people to develop more skills, get more schooling, and become a more valuable asset to our company. We felt that helping them move in a positive direction could improve their income and opportunities, and this concept was a cornerstone of our employee package."

Sam Boyer learned early that a key to growth is selecting the right people and then treating them with respect. He spent a lot of time looking for people who were flexible and could deal with the chaos of growth. He then held them accountable, kept them focused on customers and quality, valued their ideas, supported them, and helped them grow and develop. He expected them to be flexible as he tried out new ideas and built new processes and assembly lines over and around them. Likewise, he understood that his employees needed flexibility as well, and allowed them to adjust their work schedules when they had family needs. Boyer understood how to select, support, and lead the people in his company.

AIMING FOR THE FAIRWAY

Factsheet

Name:	Craig Pollard
Title:	President
Company:	Progressive Innovations, Inc.
Type of Business:	Golf products manufacturer
Location:	Vista, California
Annual Revenue:	not disclosed
Employees:	35
Years in Business:	Company founded 1994
The Edge:	Transforming into a leader and manager during explosive growth.

The Story

When Craig Pollard invented a golf product called Spike Mate, he was operating out of his garage and already had a full-time job. When he took the product to his very first trade show, one of the head buyers for Home Shopping Network saw it and bought ten to take back for evaluation. For several weeks, nothing happened. Pollard's calls to the buyer were never returned. Then one day Craig received a huge order from the buyer via his fax machine—and he had six weeks to deliver it. Pollard quit his job the next day.

"Twenty-four hours a day, seven days a week I was packaging the product to get it to Home Shopping Network; that's what launched me from being a garage-based company to a real company. I sold Spike Mate for about six months. It did really well on the Home Shopping Network and with some major mass retailers. Then I invented another product: head covers. I had a couple of sales reps selling that product in the mainstream golf market, and one of them came to me and said, 'Hey, some guys have come to me with a new product they are trying to launch called Soft Spikes. Would you be interested in distributing it?' I took a look and said 'Yeah, we'll give it a shot.'

"So we signed a contract for the exclusive rights to distribute Soft Spikes in California and Soft Spikes took off in '95 like you wouldn't believe. We shipped every Soft Spike that shipped through California for about two years and that took me from a puny company to where we are now: We stock over 1,200 products, have 35 sales reps throughout the United States, and are still adding products to the mix.

"I quickly learned that you can't grow without people. You can invent all these great products but if you don't have the right people surrounding you, you're not going anywhere. But the toughest part of growing my business was transforming myself from an inventor and marketing-type person to the leader of a distribution company with 1,200 products.

"I think the hardest thing about growth is learning how to become a leader and a manager. I'm still learning. I still have problems and probably always will, but I just keep working at it. I've learned that not everybody's personality has to be like mine. They don't have to work as hard as I do, but as long as we can work together toward common goals, we can make it work. It took me a while to realize that people have different personalities and work in different ways, but I finally learned that you can meet the goal without everybody having to be the same type of person. It took me a long time to understand that.

"I manage my sales guys differently from the warehouse guys. With the sales reps I say, 'Here's the sales goal. If you meet it or exceed it, you won't hear from me. You'll just get your check every month and that's it. And if you don't, well, you'll be hearing from me.' A new rep in a new territory will take a couple of years to establish a marketplace. I'll start putting red flags up at a year and a half if I don't start seeing some growth and some potential. And if someone's numbers aren't doing well over consecutive time periods, it's 'good bye.' I learned a lesson long ago: I'm slow to hire and quick to fire.

"I've also learned, over the years, that you can't motivate people. You can inspire them, but you can't motivate them. You have to hire people who are motivated from the beginning."

Lessons Learned

Craig Pollard learned early that it takes good people to get good results. You just can't do it with people who aren't up to the challenge, and you can't force people to be something that they aren't. Many company owners and managers think that with sufficient motivation or coaching, employees will re-mold themselves to whatever model of behavior their leaders expect. And these same owners and managers are surprised when the employee fails to meet expectations and has to be fired. Craig Pollard learned long ago that it pays to hire the right people to start with, and then to lead *them* to new heights of performance and success.

Says Pollard, "My most important lesson? You can't grow without good people. You hear that all the time. Other people tell you that's the case, and they talk about it in seminars and classes. But when you hire and get somebody who's really good and really performs, you can immediately see how much better your business is because of him or her.

Craig Pollard learned how to handle explosive growth without major breakdowns or crises. He avoided the edge by recruiting motivated people, setting goals, and holding people accountable for reaching them. He respects differences among individuals as long as everyone can work together to achieve a common goal. He rewards good performers and terminates those who don't meet expectations. In addition, he has learned to change and transform himself. He's grown from "inventor" to leader and manager of a large distribution company. Great leaders know how to change, grow, transform, and assume new roles and responsibilities when their companies evolve to a next stage of development. Pollard has learned that important lesson.

WHEN DISASTER STRIKES

Factsheet

Name:	Damon Gersh
Title:	President
Company:	Maxons Restorations, Inc.
Type of Business:	Disaster restoration
Location:	New York, New York
Annual Revenue:	$12–15 million
Employees:	25
Years in Business:	Company founded 1989
The Edge:	Overnight expansion of business, including increasing staff by 50 times the original number to help New York recover after September 11.

The Story

No one was prepared for the devastation and the tragedy that followed the September 11 terrorist attacks. Not only had an event like this never before happened on American soil, but any illusion we had that America was somehow safe from harm was suddenly and permanently shattered.

But despite the shock and disorientation that many Americans felt after the attacks, some people, agencies, and companies were prepared to respond. Their leaders had planned ahead and had developed contingencies. Their people were prepared to operate in the chaos that followed. This was vital for saving lives and bringing a sense of order, if not normalcy, back to the people and places most directly affected. One such company was Maxons Restorations, Inc.

As Damon Gersh describes the events of that fateful day, "September 11 started out as a beautiful day. On my way into the city for a leadership team meeting at our company, we heard that there was a fire at the World Trade Center. We've done work for the Port Authority, so I asked one of my project managers to make a call to our friend there to see if he needed any clean-up help once the fire was put out. And then events turned surreal when we found out about the terrorist attack and airplanes. That first day we were in shock and just wanted to be with our families and be safe. But the next day—when I saw the news reports and the collapse of the buildings and the cloud of dust that covered all of Lower Manhattan—I knew that all those buildings, apartments, offices, churches, retail stores, and restaurants would have a layer of dust all over them.

"So, being the largest disaster restoration company in Manhattan, and having the largest insured disaster in United States history happen right in the middle of our territory, we knew that we were going to be besieged by calls. We knew that we would have to brace for something unprecedented in our business.

"All of our labor is subcontracted. Although we have captive subcontractors who work exclusively for us, we have to remain flexible with our workforce because we can have a slow week and only have 100 guys working on various projects and all of a sudden we can get a high-rise fire and need 200 people for that one job. Our staff typically ranges from 100 on the low end to 400 or 500 when we're busy. We're used to having a flexible labor pool. Our own employees before September 11 numbered about 25— mostly project managers, some sales, and some administration.

"One thing I learned from attending YEO's 'Birthing of Giants' program in Boston last year with Verne Harnish was to identify and control the 'choke points' of your business. After much thought, I realized that in our company the 'choke point' was labor because we share a pool of labor that our competitors use. If we control that labor pool we control the 'choke point' of the business.

"So on September 12, our first priority was to call all of these subcontractors and secure them for our work before our competitors could call them for their work. We were proactive and we called them before we even had our first job. We said 'Either you're *on* our team or you're *against* our team. Which is it?' And these people had to make a business decision, right then, knowing that we're the largest restoration company in Manhattan and this was obviously a Manhattan loss.

"Because we don't control them as employees, we have tried to create loyalty with them. Over the years we pay them a little more and a lot faster than our competitors do. Over the years we've cultivated positive relationships with these guys so that they want to work for us. We want them to be loyal to us because we want them to work for us rather than our competitors.

"The first thing we did was to line up people. We didn't know exactly how many we would need but we knew that we would need more than we ever had before. So we called every crew, from the guys we use every day to the guys that we use once or twice a year. About 80 to 90 percent of them committed to us on that first day.

"We've done a lot of planning over the years that we didn't know would prepare us for this day, but it ultimately turned out to be crucial to our being able to work together and respond quickly. We had people who were used to making decisions, and we had guidelines that enabled the decisions to be coordinated. By the end of September, we had over 1,600 people spread out over hundreds of locations."

Lessons Learned

Planning is one of those things that every entrepreneur knows that he or she should do, but seems to avoid like the plague. Problem solving, talking with customers, and selling products and services always make the short list of fun activities; planning is seldom on the list. But planning is an incredibly powerful activity, and those who plan for the future are much better prepared to take advantage of tomorrow when it inevitably becomes today. While no one could have imagined that they would witness a tragedy on the scale of the World Trade Center Towers disaster, Maxons Restorations was prepared for a tremendous increase in customer demand. Damon Gersh was ready: Plans had been made, processes standardized, strategies identified, guidelines developed, and people trained long before the company was tested on September 11.

Says Gersh, "The single most important thing that I offered to the team was leadership, to set the tone and prioritize—to identify what's important for the company, to clarify the direction, the vision, and the values of what we're about. But I also empowered people within the organization and brought on the best people that I could get. And then I clarified the vision, gave them guidelines, and held them accountable. Beyond that, I let them exercise their creativity, bring what experience they had to the table, and trusted them to use the guidelines to make important decisions.

"Thousands of decisions were made on a daily basis that I never even knew about. Some business owners might say 'I couldn't imagine a single important decision being made without my involvement.' But others have said to me 'Where you are is where I want my company to be.'

"The day after the tragedy, another CEO might have said, 'Oh, my God. What are we going to do? We've never dealt with anything like this. We're doomed. I don't know what we're going to do.' But at the meeting on September 12 we first had a moment of silence for all the people who were lost, and then I said 'We've all been preparing our entire lives for this moment. And you know what? There's nobody more qualified to help our fellow New Yorkers than we are. We have to be focused on the task, be professional, and be considerate of the fact that these people have been traumatized. We have to make sure that our quality doesn't suffer and that we don't compromise any values or principles that we hold dear. And if we do that, we're going to make it through this.' And that's exactly what we did."

Damon Gersh did several things that enabled his company and employees to respond so quickly: He had a track record of treating subcontractors better than competitors and paying them well. So when he asked them to choose between working with him or a competitor, they chose to work with him. He had selected employees who knew how to respond quickly when a disaster struck, yet respond sensitively to the people involved. He had several managers who were ready and able to handle increased responsibilities on a moment's notice, that is, a 50-fold increase of people working on a multitude of projects requiring restoration after this incredible disaster. Gersh had planned and prepared his company to be ready for such an event. And he himself was prepared to lead his company. When the opportunity came, he saw it, seized it, and capitalized on it. He inspired his workers, he led them, and they performed at an amazing level.

Over and over, as you read this book, you'll hear entrepreneurs say, "It's all about managing and leading people." And they're right.

Your role as a leader is to select the right people, clarify the vision, and develop systems and procedures that they can all use to make decisions. Then, let them do their job. Let them use their expertise, apply their experience, operate within the guidelines and make decisions about how best to serve the customer.

ALWAYS BEHIND THE CURVE

Factsheet

Name:	Howard Getson
Title:	Founder and Board Member
Company:	IntellAgent Control
Type of Business:	Sales force automation
Location:	Coppell, Texas
Annual Revenue:	$8.5 million
Employees:	100
Years in Business:	Company founded 1991
The Edge:	No accountability, inexperienced management causing huge opportunity costs and struggle to survive.

The Story

Howard Getson founded his company—IntellAgent Control—with two other practicing attorneys on April Fool's Day, 1991. The original idea was to provide technology services to law firms. However, they quickly found that law firms weren't as interested in technology or efficiency as they thought they would be. So they shifted the focus of the company to the production of sales force automation software.

Says Getson, "I made a couple of mistakes that are now really clear to me. I was the consummate visionary entrepreneur who could see clearly 18 months out but wasn't looking at today or tomorrow. I loved meeting with clients and going to product specification or client meetings, but I didn't enjoy the day-to-day reality of running a growing business. Because we had done so well, our momentum, money, and increasing revenue hid the fact that there was a cancer creeping into the workplace. Our culture was eroding because people weren't held accountable and they could hide."

The company's business operations were becoming increasingly sophisticated and complex, but the people that Getson had hired into key management positions couldn't keep up, and their inability to do so caused the company to miss out on a number of opportunities.

He never quite had the right management to take the company to the next level. "We were always a layer behind. When I had 35 employees, my head of sales and marketing, my head of consulting, my head of technology were all good. But the best employee when we had 17 employees was probably only a reasonably good employee when I had 40, and probably average or below when we had 70. We had scaled past their capability to grow when we got above that. And that happened over and over. We were always behind the curve. Our head of sales was a terrific head of sales for a million dollar company, was an OK head of sales at $5 million, but couldn't ever be the vice president of sales and marketing at a public company. He was a great person, but the company and market had outgrown his capability. Ultimately I figured out that we would have been much better off if I had hired a COO (chief operating officer) who understood all this; who knew who to hire, how to hold people accountable; who knew when to hire, replace, fire; and who could build a senior management team."

Lessons Learned

Unfortunately, Getson didn't have the right people systems in place. He hadn't put in the infrastructure to get the right people in the right job, measure their performance, set stretch goals, coach them to a higher level of performance, hold them accountable, determine whether they were right for the job, and if not, let them go. This is a hard lesson for most entrepreneurs.

Jacques Habra, an entrepreneur with similar experiences, founded Web Elite, an e-business consulting and development firm. Jacques started his company when he was in college and invited some former classmates to work with him. After hiring an operations manager from outside his initial group, Habra was stunned when his employees made a grab for his company. He realized he'd done a bad job of hiring, leading, and managing people. Habra says, "I've learned that if you don't have experience and aren't good at it, don't do it. Hire someone else to do it. I hadn't been around the block regarding hiring and managing people, so I should have surrounded myself with the most talented, experienced people and empowered them to do it, rather than try to do it myself."

NO SYSTEM, NO RESULTS

Factsheet

Name:	Alex Rusch
Title:	Publisher
Company:	Rusch Publishing
Type of Business:	Audio book publisher
Location:	Zurich, Switzerland
Annual Revenue:	not disclosed
Employees:	10
Years in Business:	Company founded 1994
The Edge:	Rapid hiring resulting in declines in efficiency and customer service. Lack of processes and protocols caused poor performance.

The Story

Rusch Publishing, founded in 1994 by Alex Rusch, is one of Europe's top publishers of audio books in the areas of self-help and management. Many of the company's audio books are best-selling American books, including *Don't Sweat the Small Stuff*, *Chicken Soup for the Soul*, *Fit for Life*, and others. Rusch also publishes books and magazines and conducts seminars under a number of other company names. But while the company is enjoying great success today, getting there hasn't been an easy process, particularly when it came to finding and hiring people who were as dedicated to the success of his company as he was.

Says Rusch, "At every stage, I've had adversity. But hiring and managing people has almost driven me to the edge. When you first start a business, it's a one-man show. Then you start to grow the company and hire the people, and suddenly you've got staff problems. Usually, the people you hire at the beginning are not that efficient. Before you know it, you've got all these people working here, and you've got no efficiency. You've got no quality in customer service. You've got all these problems. I had to spend a lot more time wording my help-wanted ads and doing interviews. We learned not to hire people until they've worked with us for a couple of days and demonstrated their skills and their fit with the company. And in Switzerland, there's a three-month probation before you definitely hire anyone, so that helped."

To grow your business, you have to hire employees. There is only so much value you can create by yourself, so hiring employees allows you to multiply the potential value of your company many times, creating an engine of growth that can quickly propel your company forward. However, when you begin to hire employees, you need to create an infrastructure of systems and policies to guide their efforts. In the early days of his business, Alex Rusch didn't recognize the importance of management systems and controls and he feels his employees took advantage of the situation.

"I found that I needed to be tougher, not so easygoing. If you're always a nice guy, if you don't set goals or have any expectations, people work less; people are less productive; people are less efficient. Our business was growing, but I became certain that we were making less money because we had so many people here, and they were not that productive. Certain things just weren't getting done, even though we had enough people. I know how long everything takes because I did everything myself in the beginning. I was a one-man show. I know how long all the processing takes, how long it takes to make a parcel, how long accounting takes. I've done everything in the past. Suddenly I noticed that we've got all these people, but they don't get their work done. Things just sit on their desks. Certain things are just not getting done, even though they've had enough time to do them."

Lessons Learned

"One of the lessons I've learned is that we need to have a company manual and an operations manual. You need to have things written down. A manual that describes all the steps in all our processes—step one, step two, step three, and so on—makes it easier to explain to people how we do things and helps them not to forget anything. The manual needs to be something that people can easily read and easily apply. That's been a big help.

"We have also developed some systems to track goals and assess productivity. For instance, we track incoming phone calls. Every employee is required to write down all the phone calls that come in that they answer. First, that enables me to learn who called and why they were calling. Second, I can see how many people called when I look at all the sheets of the day. When employees tell me they didn't get their work done because the phone rang too often, I can say, 'That's not really true; it didn't ring that often. Look at your sheet. You only picked up ten phone calls yesterday. That's no excuse for not getting your work done.' And when the volume of calls picks up, I can tell from the sheet, and then I can decide whether we need to hire someone else. I don't like too much administration, but there are certain policies, procedures and forms that you need to manage your company.

"I need to have employees. There's no other way because we need the people at the phone; we need to have people who sell. But you have to feed all these people. You have to pay them salaries. And when you feel they don't put in enough effort to justify that salary, you have to act quickly to change their behavior or you have to let them go.

"At the beginning of the year I hired a customer services manager who used to work for a large corporation, but I had to fire her after two months because she couldn't change her large company mentality. She was used to being in meetings all day and she kept wanting to have meetings. We are a very small company, and everybody here has to work. I have to work. We can't just sit in meetings all day long.

"I had to fire somebody last week who was here for only six weeks. He was very unproductive. I warned him, but it didn't get any better. In the past, I probably would have kept that person three or four months just to see what would happen—hoping for improvement. But now, I don't wait that long. I can tell a lot faster if somebody is going to work out. I knew that he would never be productive. So I fired him after six weeks. It just needed to be done. You can't just wait, and you can't just hope. It's difficult if you have to fire somebody and that person becomes unemployed; it was real tough for me last week. But it had to be done in the interest of the company."

Alex Rusch has learned that people are essential to his success, but they need to be managed and led. He learned to take more time hiring people and trying them out. He now sets goals and has developed a company manual and an operations manual that describe the various steps in the process. He tracks activities, assesses individual performance, provides feedback, warns employees whose performance doesn't meet his standards, then fires those who aren't able or willing to perform. Rusch found that better management systems enabled his employees to be more productive and his company to be more profitable. And when he determines the people will not work out in his company, he doesn't wait a long time to fire them. Some might say Rusch is harsh when he says, "You can't wait. You can't hope. . . . It has to be done in the interest of the company." But if you want to be successful and grow, you have to hire and develop a team of people who share your company's values and will perform according to your expectations. If you have hired the wrong people, you need to follow due process, and then let them go. If you don't fire them, you send the wrong signal to those employees who are working hard and share your values, and they will become de-motivated. If you don't fire poor performers, your company's performance will be negatively affected. And if you do fire them, they have an opportunity to look for another company that's a better fit with their values, performance capabilities, and career aspirations.

PICKING THE WRONG GUY . . . AGAIN

Factsheet

Name:	Paul Hickey
Title:	CEO
Company:	Q Comm International, Inc.
Type of Business:	Prepaid telecommunications service provider
Location:	Orem, Utah
Annual Revenue:	$24 million
Employees:	24
Years in Business:	Company founded 1992
The Edge:	Hiring the wrong candidate for president three times in a row; resulting in new problems each time.

The Story

Paul Hickey started Q Comm International in 1992 as an interactive voice response (IVR) service bureau. After working for other IVR service bureaus and creating successful marketing programs, Hickey woke up one day and decided to start his own business. Says Hickey, "I decided I could provide a better product and a better service. I had the money to go do it myself, and it didn't take a lot, so I just funded it and got it going. It was just 'being at the right place at the right time.'"

The company showed steady increases in revenue and profit in 1993 and 1994, but things started getting a bit challenging in 1995 as Hickey pushed to expand his company. "I had worked for two small fast-growth companies that went from a few million dollars to fifty million in sales within two years and were bankrupt the third year. Both of them had the same problem. The entrepreneur who had the vision understood how to get the thing up and running, but neither of these smart entrepreneurs was a great manager, and they didn't get out of the way. So I said, 'I'm not making that mistake. I'm bringing in professional managers right from the beginning, the minute I start making a decent profit.' And I did that. But the way I went about bringing in the top management is where I went wrong and that's what literally cost me millions of dollars.

"I didn't want to hire a headhunter to bring in candidates because I didn't want to spend the $30,000 bucks or whatever. I thought, 'That's outrageous. I can run ads all over the place for $5,000, get a zillion leads, and interview them myself.' And I did that—three times before I realized I needed a professional involved to help me to hire the right person. Fortunately, the fourth time we got Dave, the guy who is president of my company right now and who's been just unbelievably great, and he came to us through a headhunter. We could never have gotten to where we are today without him.

"I hired three presidents myself, none of them worked out, and each time something different was wrong about them. And each time, it took me a different period of time to figure out what was wrong and to take action. The first guy I hired was *really* good at covering stuff up, at covering up problems. I guess that was a function of his being a manager in a large corporation for so many years; he had learned how to do that. That one took me over a year to figure out. I think a lot of entrepreneurs do what I did. You bring in someone you think is talented to take care of business and all the stuff you don't like, and you're so glad to get rid of it that you walk away too soon. You're so glad to get away from all the day-to-day details that you turn over your responsibilities a lot more quickly than you should. And that gives your new manager the opportunity to hide things.

"The next time I hired someone, I offered profit-sharing so he'd have some financial risk—and reward. I think that's very important when you are bringing in top-level management, particularly a president. But that guy turned out to be somebody who couldn't deal with pressure. When we hired him, we weren't on easy street any more. The company was starting to have some challenges, so I ended up restructuring, shutting down a couple of small divisions, and we started to launch new product lines. There was a lot of pressure, and he did not perform well under pressure. So he had to go.

"The next guy to come in had very good credentials from a company that was very similar to ours, and I thought, 'Okay, great.' But he was what I would classify as a sales promoter personality. Those guys are really good at selling you on their ideas and selling you on how great all their programs are going to work, and they oversell everything and under-deliver everything. That's a real dangerous personality to put in as president of a company, because that's exactly what he did: over-promised and under-delivered. Nothing worked as well as he advertised it would, and we ended up spending a lot of money on things that didn't pan out.

"So that led me to my current president, who came to me when we were in a complete turnaround mode. He had done four previous turnarounds and had a background working in large corporations. He had worked for GE Capital in one of their divisions, and then he got hired by a venture capitalist to go turn around a company, which he did. So I thought, 'This guy is perfect.' We set up a real nice stock option program for him so his incentives were lined up with mine as an owner, and we've never looked back."

Lessons Learned

Finding and recruiting a talented executive team becomes increasingly important if you want to manage and accelerate growth. Unfortunately, few founder/owners have the skills, experience, or the expertise to do this, much less to do it well. The result is hiring mistakes that can cripple the growth of a company.

Hickey said. "I should have hired and spent the 30 grand on a recruiting company six years ago. That's what they do full time, and if they bring in the wrong person, they've got to replace the person for free. There is a big difference between somebody who's coming to you who's *looking* for a job versus somebody the recruiter finds who's *doing* a good job. That's a big distinction. Top-quality search firms can find people who are really talented, like the guy who is here right now. I should have gone to a headhunter right from the beginning, and that's what I'll do the next time I start a business."

Doug Mellinger (who is featured in section 1 on Leadership) agrees with Paul Hickey and also wishes he had used outside help to recruit top management. "I would definitely use a search firm. We did not do so for many of our senior people, and I now think it was a mistake. You need to have as broad a pool as possible to pick from, and I think search firms can cast a broader net. They do a good job for those critical positions. Search firms are expensive, but it's more expensive not to have them. I had to pay millions of dollars in severance fees to get rid of the wrong people."

But remember that the search firm only identifies promising candidates. You still have to do the hard work of determining which candidate will do the best job in your company. As Mellinger reminds us, "Once you get some good candidates, you have to ask questions to determine whether they have the right leadership qualities, how hands-on they will be, and how they will take action. And finally, you need to be sure to do the background and reference checks."

As Hickey thinks about his lessons learned, he says, "I had the right idea—to get out of the way and bring in good management as the company grew. But I didn't bring in good management. I brought in mediocre management, and to make things worse, I let them go six months to a year before I did anything about it. In retrospect, here's what I should have done: We should have been joined at the hip for the first 30 days, and I would have given the person a very strong, detailed performance review at the end of 30 days. Then I would have had a very close tie the next 60 days and would have worked with the person on a daily basis. Finally, I would have scheduled a debriefing with the person every single day for the first 90 days, because—remember—it's *your* company. I don't care if you bring in a president that likes to have autonomy and says he's going to make things happen. They all tell you that, but it's not their company and it's not their money. You've got to remember that.

"I kept thinking, 'It's so great to have somebody here who can take these management problems off my back.' I got excited by the thought that it was really going to happen, and I let go much too soon. I finally learned my lesson on that one."

Paul Hickey made several mistakes. First, he did not hire the right person—three times—for the job of president. Many first-time entrepreneurs make the mistake of hiring someone to take on the roles and responsibilities of the person who just departed. But in a growing company, the roles and responsibilities are constantly changing. So each time Hickey should have hired someone who would be able to assume a new set of roles and responsibilities, not the old ones. If you haven't done this before, it's difficult to get it right, and this is why you need outside experts. Second, he made the mistake of "dumping" or "handing off" the management responsibilities, then walking away. He now realizes it should have been a gradual process of delegation: first, testing the person, coaching him or her, delegating, reviewing performance, delegating more, reviewing performance, coaching over a 90-day period before fully delegating those roles and responsibilities to the new president. His third mistake was not setting clear goals and holding the person accountable. A good leader would not have allowed the first president to "cover up" things or the third president to "overpromise and underdeliver". Hickey should have set goals, measured progress on a timetable, and held people accountable. And finally, as he admits, he did not make changes quickly enough when he recognized that the person was not performing as president. As Chris Rosica, President of Rosica-Mulhern PR Agency, notes, "I've never heard anyone say that they fired someone too soon, but I've heard a lot of people say they waited too long." When it's clear that there is an issue of values or a performance problem, don't dither. Act.

≈ Wrap-up ≈

The entrepreneurs in this section do not have a corner on the "people stories." There are stories all through the book that emphasize the importance of selecting the right people, managing and leading them to do their work and perform at their best. If you're going to build a company for growth, you must develop policies and procedures, systems and processes, checks and balances that will enable your people to perform at their best. Contrary to what many entrepreneurs believe, these organizational systems do not inhibit your growth. A solid infrastructure actually enables you to accelerate growth.

Think about whether you have appropriate people systems in place in your company. Think about the kinds of people you have selected. Are they flexible, adaptable, do they take risks, innovate, and keep learning? Do they share your values, your entrepreneurial spirit and drive? Do they hit deadlines and do things right—the first time? Do the members of your top team have good skills and experience in customer management, crisis management and people management? Do you have the right people in place to take your company to the next level of growth or are you behind the curve and closer to the edge than you'd think?

Chris Rosica, President of Rosica-Mulhern, an advertising and public relations firm is not only diligent about the hiring process, he tries to make sure to put people in positions where they will perform well. Two years ago he realized that his second largest expenditure was headhunters fees. "Finding the right people has been a huge challenge for us. I know that in order to achieve our growth plans, we have to attract and retain talented people. To make sure we have the right people in the right position, I am now utilizing a personality and work preference survey. I have a consultant who helps me evaluate each of my staff to make sure that their jobs and duties are consistent with their personality and work preferences. And since I can't afford to bring in the wrong people, I'm giving the test to prospective employees as well as existing ones to make sure I am getting the right people in the right positions.

"I've also changed my management focus. I used to be hands off when people demonstrated their ability to excel and achieve results and was more hands-on with people who were struggling. But now I'm spending more time with the high performers. I'm trying to learn from people who are achieving these terrific results. I am not spending nearly as much time with people who don't. If it's a skill that I need to teach, I need to know what it is and figure out how to help other people learn it. But if it's a personality or values issue, or if they aren't as driven or organized as they need to be, then I shouldn't hire them in the first place. And if I've already hired them, they need to go."

Chris Rosica has learned that his job is not just to hire the right people, but to match them up with positions in which they excel. He now spends more of his time with the high performers, tries to figure out why they are successful, then tries to teach and coach others. But if he has some employees who are not performing up to expectations, he doesn't "hope" things improve; he takes appropriate action.

In the next section we'll address Partnership issues. Partnerships, like marriages, are very easy to get into but quite painful and expensive to get out of. After reviewing the Ten Lessons on People, keep reading and learn how to avoid the partnership edge.

Top Ten Lessons on People

1. Hire people who share your values and make sure they understand that they can reach their goals by helping you and your company reach its goals.

2. Look for people who are flexible, adaptable, willing to take risks, innovative, comfortable with change, and want to keep learning. They are the people who will propel your company's growth.

3. Make sure that you hire self-motivated people. Don't hire anyone—or keep anyone—that you have to motivate.

4. If you're trying to grow, hire people who will help take your company to the next level, rather than replacing the person who just left or filling a current position that's open.

5. Do not hire people who are clones of you or expect everyone to do it your way. Value diversity, and learn to manage different types of people.

6. Hire to your weaknesses. If you are the visionary, make sure you hire some people who excel in the day-to-day work. If accounting is not a skill, hire a CFO and then have an outside audit conducted on a regular basis.

7. If you're not good at recruiting and don't know what to look for, hire people who know more than you do to help you, or use a recruiting firm to find good candidates.

8. Provide guidelines that describe the parameters within which people can operate, then let them exercise their creativity, apply their expertise, and hold them accountable for achieving results.

9. Set goals, measure progress, and reward those that perform. Spend more time with your high achievers than your low performers.

10. Learn to delegate, but not abdicate. Do not hire someone or promote someone, then walk away and expect him or her to perform well. Work with them, at successively higher level of delegation, until you are satisfied the person is ready and able to take on the full responsibility of the job.

≈ Partnerships ≈

Section-at-a-Glance

Overview

Individual Profiles

Profile: Jeff Dennis
The Edge: Real estate market crash forced a harsh decision on whether to continue; had to deal with partners who had different goals.

Profile: Julie Pearl
The Edge: Partner kept renegotiating deal without an agreement; management clash between partners created large liability.

Profile: David Dash
The Edge: A serious conflict of interest by one partner forced an arbitrator to decide whether the entrepreneur would lose or keep his company.

Profile: Peter Davies
The Edge: Stuck between two warring partners, the entrepreneur faced personal liability for their actions.

Profile: Mike Meek
The Edge: Partner falsified credentials, caused personal loss and
                embarrassment, forced company to rename.

Profile: Greg Ferguson
The Edge: Incompatible values, lifestyles, and plans for the
                company forced partners to break up the company.

Profile: Tina Holden
The Edge: Owner gave away part of company with little in
                return; lost control of company.

Wrap-up

Top Ten Lessons in Partnerships

≈ Partnerships ≈
Overview

When people start a company, they often feel that they don't have all the skills, contacts, or capital needed to grow it. One or more partners can help compensate for any shortfalls you yourself may have in a particular area. For example, you might be great at selling, but not so great at managing employees. Or you may have a great idea, but not enough money to launch a business. Finding a partner who can complement you—providing expertise and resources where yours are lacking—can put the company on the road to success.

But partnerships can, and sometimes do, go wrong. When that happens, your business, your personal finances, your relationships with family and friends, your reputation, and even your health can be put in jeopardy.

In this section, you'll read the stories of a number of entrepreneurs who found out that their partner and the partnership was not what they bargained for. Julie Pearl had a partner who never signed the partnership documents, decided she wanted a much bigger piece of the pie than they had originally discussed, then left quite a mess when she departed. In his own business, *Lessons from the Edge* co-author Jeff Dennis found to his chagrin that partners often have different expectations. If those differences are not identified early and somehow resolved, they can lead to major disappointments as the company grows and people "check out." There are some very ugly stories of partners who didn't deliver, who failed to carry their share of the load, or who were just plain dishonest.

Partnerships can turn out to be the best decision—or the worst decision—you will ever make. They can be good or they can be bad, depending on the person you choose as a partner; whether you share the same goals, values, and expectations for the partnership; the legal safeguards you put in place when you set up the partnership; and whether each partner believes that the agreement, allocation of responsibilities, and the risks and rewards are fair and equitable.

As you read these stories, think about the following questions:

- Did people take the time to get to know their prospective partners or did they jump into the partnership without a lot of thought or discussion? Partnerships, like marriages, are easy to get into and can be very messy to get out of.

- Would you be willing to trust your life—and your future—to this partner? High growth is a lot like white-water rapids. Sharing a business with a partner is like being on a raft. You try to paddle and steer, but it often feels out of control. You want to make sure that your partner will keep cool, coordinate efforts with you, and do his or her share of the paddling. And if you happen to fall out of the raft, you want to know that person will do everything in his or her power to rescue you and keep the raft afloat. You don't want to be in the middle of the white-water, wondering whether you partner has the "right stuff."

- What happens when partners don't share the same integrity and ethics?

- Are your partner's goals for the business similar to yours? Do you share similar values about life?

- Is there agreement on how to lead and manage a company?

- Do you and your partners have a sound legal document that spells out an exit strategy if "the worst" happens—for example, a partner dies, embezzles, or simply wants out of the partnership?

Mike Meek, CEO of Intellitec, didn't learn the truth about his partner until after he brought him into his company. And not only had this partner lied, but he racked up large debts that Meek was obligated to pay off.

> I lost a significant amount of money in that partnership. At the end of the day, the guy was a con man. We ended up closing down the company. That was my first experience with people who will actually lie to you.

Many partners think they can get by on a handshake and are then surprised that they're burned when a partnership goes bad. Developing good shareholder and partnership agreements from the very start is one way to protect yourself from getting burned. Partners can change for a variety of reasons. No one can predict fully the impact of life-changing events like illness, divorce, or bankruptcy on a partner. Sometimes the temptations of envy, avarice, and greed are too much for them to handle.

Louette Glabb (whom you will meet in section 5) and her partner divided up the responsibilities. She was responsible for sales and he was responsible for the financial affairs of the company. He began moving profits into the company's savings account, and from there into a stock account. He invested the money without discussing any of this with Louette, then moved some of it into his personal savings account. He started writing checks to himself—believing that he deserved the money. When she discovered he had embezzled over a hundred thousand dollars, she made a proposal: She would not press charges if he would sign over his share of the company.

Abelardo Cruz, President of Imagen Contemporanea in Monterey, Mexico, built a company that designs and outfits office space that is now Steelcase's strategic partner in Mexico. In retrospect, he found that he had overvalued his partners' contribution when he shared stock:

When I started the company, I realized I needed help, and I chose three people who I thought had the talent to come in and help me run the business. I gave them each 25 percent ownership, but one day they said they would no longer accept me as general manager, that we should all be equals. I was very naïve about handling my relationships with partners and colleagues. I invented the business and put in all the capital. In retrospect I overvalued their contributions when I gave them equal shares. I did not take into account who would be contributing what to the long-term growth of the business.

In many cases, entrepreneurs have the mistaken belief that just because someone is older, has more experience, has money to invest, has an MBA, or has strength in areas in which they are weak, the person is also honest and will have the entrepreneur's best interests at heart. Tina Holden, like Cruz, was trusting and naïve. People she thought would be partners bought into her company. They took control, then began withholding her paychecks. According to Holden,

> I gave up controlling interest of the company. I thought my partner was going to bring in somebody to help me run the company, but my partners decided to pull the rug right out from underneath my feet.

Don't rush into a partnership. Think of it as a business marriage. You and your partner(s) will end up spending a large portion of your waking hours together. Decisions your partner will make will have an impact on the company and its reputation, as well as your own. If you're going to share your life, your money, your dream, and your reputation with someone else, you had better be sure it's the right fit *before* you and the person become partners—not after. Entrepreneur Ralf Mandt-Rauch, founder of MCMT and Europawatch.com, advises that you be 100 percent sure that you and your partner are on the same wavelength, and then make sure that your interests are aligned and stay aligned. He found that this was not nearly as easy as it sounds.

Build in buffers—for example, work together for a time before becoming formal partners. Have some heavy-duty conversations. Do some reference checks, get a credit report; in other words, be diligent in researching the background of your potential partner. In some cases, you may even want to do a criminal records check.

Even if you've known someone since high school, take a hard look at the person through the lenses of a business partner.

In the stories that follow, we focus on the perils of partnerships. Obviously not every partnership is fated to go bad. But even partnerships that start well, with the best of intentions, can go bad if you don't manage them and plan for their ending. The good news is that there are some clear steps you can take to ensure that you don't end up in the same situation as the CEOs in our stories. Read on to learn their lessons from the partnership edge.

Individual Profiles

STARTING WITH A BANG, ENDING WITH A WHIMPER

Factsheet

Name:	Jeff Dennis
Title:	Managing Director
Company:	Ashton-Royce Capital Corporation
Type of Business:	Creating, distributing, and managing sophisticated financial investments
Location:	Toronto, Ontario
Annual Revenue:	$300 million (CDN)
Employees:	7
Years in Business:	Company founded 1989; closed in 1998; 9 years
The Edge:	Real estate market crash forced a harsh decision on whether to continue; had to deal with partners who had different goals.

The Story

Having partners can be a real asset to a business, particularly when each partner brings something that the other partners are missing: money, expertise, customers, or contacts. But what happens when one of your partners decides that he or she has worked hard enough and is ready to enjoy the fruits of all that labor while the other partners want more and continue to work their tails off? This is clearly a recipe for discontent.

Jeff Dennis co-founded Ashton-Royce Capital Corporation in May 1989 with three other partners. "I had a longer-standing relationship with Grant—we were classmates in law school—so he and I knew each other well, trusted each other, and worked well together. The other two guys came from sales backgrounds. They had been stockbrokers and weren't really interested in the administrative side of the business. All they wanted to do was sell, make money, and have fun. Our initial business involved the syndication of commercial real estate. We would tie up properties with a small deposit, and then we would find investors to put up the cash before we had to close the deal. We never missed a closing!

"Grant and I ran the business. I am a lawyer by trade, so I negotiated all the purchase agreements, dealt with the attorneys, and conceived the structure of each deal. And when deals closed, Grant and I provided all the management services. We weren't paid extra for that per se; we were all equal partners. At first it really wasn't an issue for me because we were making a lot of money. I was 31 years old, and I thought I had died and gone to heaven.

"But after we started making real money, one of the partners hit his 'number' and effectively stopped working. He began spending four months a year in California in semiretirement. Another partner followed his lead. But even as they became less and less involved in the day-to-day operations of the business, they wanted the right to second-guess Grant and me, and they resented the fact that Grant and I were seen as the leaders of the business. But we *were* the business; they were just the sales guys. And Grant and I began to resent their rapidly declining contributions to the firm.

"We got our first wake-up call when the real estate market crashed in the early '90s, and we were effectively out of business. We quickly came to the conclusion we just couldn't cut it anymore, and we had to make some kind of decision. Either we were going to split up, and I was going to go back and practice law, or we were going to figure out a new business to be in. We went through a kind of paradigm shift, but these two partners were really resisting it. One of them kept saying: 'We're in the real estate business, we're in the real estate business,' and Grant and I said, 'No, no—we're in the business of raising money. Real estate happens to be the commodity du jour. If we can raise money for real estate in this economy, in this climate when nobody wants it, imagine what we can raise for something people actually want. Let's go figure it out.'

"In Ontario in those days, interest rates were quite high, the real estate market was very depressed, the economy was in recession, and you couldn't raise risk capital. So we started looking at tax shelters—television and film deals—because they offered a way to help people save more of the money they were making. Our combined federal and provincial tax rates in Canada, at that time, were approaching 54 percent. We decided that instead of reinventing the wheel—figuring out a tax shelter game on our own—we'd try to align ourselves with somebody with some expertise and experience and get up that learning curve quickly. And so we found a new partner. We agreed to do a fairly small deal with him as a test, on an agency basis, and then we all agreed that if it worked out, we'd become partners. So, we did a small deal—under CA$3.3 million—and we did it in under 30 days.

"For him to tie up a whole deal and rely on us to show up with all the money was a huge risk for him at the time. We were joking with him, 'Don't worry, we'll show up with everything in a nice, neat bow.' In fact, at closing, we showed up with the money, and the subscription forms, and the checks gift-wrapped with a nice neat bow. We still laugh about it. We did CA$10 million in the first year and CA$30 million in the second year, and then we did CA$100 million, CA$200 million, and the last year the tax shelter was over CA$300 million. We sold that business, and last year the same business with the new owner will do close to CA$600 million.

"Ultimately, our original partnership ended with a whimper, not a bang. While we had a shareholder's agreement with the usual clauses in it, Grant and I felt that most of the client relationships that existed were personal to us. And while there was a lot of good-will in the company and its name, Grant and I felt we could start under a new moniker without missing a beat. On the other hand, we felt the other two partners would benefit unduly if they were allowed to retain the company and its name, especially consider-ing the way that they had 'checked out' of the business. The result was that we decided to simply 'retire' the old company. Nobody could use the name, and both groups would start fresh."

Lessons Learned

To ensure the success of an enterprise, there has to be a real syn-ergy among the partners. Unfortunately, this is something much easier said than done, especially if there are more than two part-ners. In Jeff Dennis's case, the different goals and personal lifestyles of two of his partners became a liability to the business and seri-ously damaged the partnership. While it is difficult to know in advance how your partners will react to the success of your com-pany, it is in your interest to ensure that the values of prospective partners are completely in sync with yours—before you invite them to join your firm. This requires substantial research: interviews, reference checks, and due diligence.

Says Jeff Dennis, "Get to know who you are getting into business with. Business is like a marriage. It's easy to get into a partnership, but it can be messy getting out. Make sure that your partners have similar ambitions, values, and timelines. Review your goals regularly to make sure that you continue to share the same perspective. An-ticipate your egress route—shotgun buyout, third-party sale, public offering, or some other creative way out. It's part of the 'get-to-know-you' discussions you need to have. Those are the kinds of questions that you've got to ask one another, issues you've got to explore. It's not enough to have the same business idea; it's issues of values, ambition, and culture that will make or break a partnership. If you're going to butt heads on those basic things, you'll never get along. My mother always said, 'The friends you keep are a reflection on you.' That's even more true with a business partnership."

GET IT IN WRITING

Factsheet

Name:	Julie Pearl
Title:	Managing Attorney and CEO
Company:	Munro, Nelson & Pearl
Type of Business:	Immigration legal services
Location:	San Francisco, California
Annual Revenue:	not disclosed
Employees:	not disclosed
Years in Business:	Company founded 1994
The Edge:	Partner kept renegotiating deal without an agreement; management clash between partners created large liability.

The Story

Just a few years out of law school, Julie Pearl started her firm with two partners—the former head of the Immigration Service under presidents Reagan and Bush, and an established immigration law attorney. Since opening up an office in San Francisco, the firm had grown to be one of the six largest immigration law firms in northern California. A few years after starting up her firm, Julie decided to bring in another partner but, as she soon found out, you can't make someone into something that he or she isn't. You have to learn to assess a person for who that person is.

Says Pearl, "She signed on for 5 percent. A year later, I got pregnant and I wanted her to hold down the fort, so I bumped her up to 10 percent of the profit sharing. We never did finish the partnership agreement, in part because she had a whole bunch of questions about a variety of different issues.

"She felt that we should add her name to the firm's name, even though we hadn't yet signed the partnership agreement. I really trusted her and believed we were close on the partnership agreement, so I agreed to do it; and we changed the name. Then, about three months later, she said, 'By the way, I want 50 percent and the right to veto anybody else getting profit sharing.'

"There was no way that I was going to give her 50 percent. In April, she told me we weren't going ahead with the partnership agreement; then, in early July, she gave notice. I found out later that between April and July, while she was focused on her job search, one of the paralegals she supervised stole from a client.

"We've never had anything like that happen in all these years. The paralegal had experience at the biggest immigration firm in the country, and we thought his references checked out. But she should have noticed that there was something wrong. He said he had filed a particular case, but he couldn't have filed it without her. She didn't use our systems or make him use our systems. There's a report he has to print every two weeks. She let months go by without his reporting.

"I had no qualms about her ability to do the law, but as a manager, she was just beyond bad because she didn't hold anyone accountable. So after she left, we ended up with a big, big, mess. We now have $90,000 of liability. About $20,000 we had to pay out of pocket. On top of that, she sent us a demand for $75,000 as her share of more of the profits.

"We went months without my really knowing what she wanted in terms of a partnership. I should have realized that behavior like that was never going to be a good fit for me. I just didn't know how bad a fit it would be. This was somebody I thought I was close to. I made her one of my bridesmaids. Every other bridesmaid had been somebody I'd known for years and years. In this case, I just jumped in too far.

"I had anticipated a whole bunch of problems when I started the company: Would I have enough clients, make enough money, achieve my bottom-line goals—all the things you worry about. But I never anticipated the loneliness I felt. So I wanted somebody else here to share responsibility for decisions on how much we pay people, flexible hours, and all that stuff. I wanted so much to have a partner that I tried to make somebody into one who wasn't."

Lessons Learned

If Julie Pearl learned anything from her troubling experience with her "almost" partner, it was that she should remain first of all true to herself. Pearl tried to make her "partner" into someone she wasn't because Pearl wanted her to work out as a partner for her business. Rather than judging the person on her strengths and weaknesses, Pearl assumed she would work out and became overly committed to the person—asking her to be a bridesmaid and even putting her name on the door as a partner—before a partnership agreement was signed. As it turned out, this failed partner would have been a tremendous liability to the firm had she gained true partner status.

Says Pearl, "Your basic core values shouldn't change. If you value something like 'always stay really open about what's going on,' then do not even pass 'go' with somebody who's not that way. Don't say, 'Well, I should be open to other ways of doing things.' Just say, 'You know what, I'm the given here. This has to work for me.'

"And if you're bringing in a partner simply because you're lonely, find other ways to satisfy your needs. Join a CEO group, Young Entrepreneurs' Organization, or some other peer group. Don't force somebody to be a partner when that person is just not ready. You want to have a sense that your partner will care about the company as much as you do.

"But no matter how hard you screen, you still don't know if it's really going to be a fit. There are so many variables. So be patient. Work together a couple of years to see how it goes, and then consider a partnership."

A MATTER OF INTERPRETATION

Factsheet

Name:	David Dash
Title:	President
Company:	Dash Wireless Communications Inc.
Type of Business:	Wireless Telecommunications Services
Location:	Vancouver, British Columbia
Annual Revenue:	$1.5 million
Employees:	15
Years in Business:	Company founded 1995
The Edge:	A serious conflict of interest by one partner, resulting in the other partner seeking an arbitrator's decision as to whether or not he would lose or keep his company.

The Story

While working as a salesman for Rogers AT&T, David Dash met a man who owned a majority share of a wireless communications company. The man wanted to expand his company into a number of retail locations, so he developed five stores, created partnerships, and looked for owners who would take 50 percent of the individual stores. Dash liked the concept and bought 50 percent of one of the stores. So far, so good, but the fun had just begun.

According to David Dash, "My job was to operate the retail store, drive sales and manage the staff. His job—the job of his company that had a stake in each of the partnerships—was essentially to do the accounting, maintain the information systems, and to deal directly with the carrier, BCTel Mobility, now known as Telus Mobility, on behalf of the separate stores. He was supposed to provide us with up-to-date financial information, but he never did that—he was in constant and complete chaos in terms of his ability to provide us with proper accounting, financial statements, and the transactions between the two companies.

"For example the idea was to get inventory cheaper by buying as a group. We would send our orders into the head office (his company), they would then order for everybody, and send the inventory to us. We were to pay for that inventory by offsetting the inventory purchase from the payments that went to him from the carrier on our behalf. The balance would be paid to our company, the company that made the sales. But if you are never provided with proper accounting information, you never know if you're getting what you're supposed to get out of the deal.

"Eventually, this guy decided to stop sending one of his other partners, who unlike me had been receiving funds from him, any more payments from the carrier. He was told that he had a cash flow problem. In the shareholder's agreements, there was a mechanism to go to arbitration. The other store owner decided to do that, and he later brought me on board as well to share the cost. We shared the lawyer and took the action together. The arbitration took almost two years and was quite costly. This was one of the most difficult periods in my life.

"In the end, we won each of the major points that were brought against him, and our mutual partner was forced to pay each of us. We had to serve a number of garnishing orders in order to get paid, but I did end up getting paid about 90 percent of more than $100,000 over a period of two years."

Lessons Learned

As David Dash learned, when it comes to partnerships, written agreements are *everything*. But it's not enough to just have an agreement; you've got to have access to financial records, and you need to affiliate with someone who doesn't have cash flow problems of their own. When David Dash became a 50/50 partner with a man who owned 100 percent of the parent franchise, he found out too late that the parent didn't have the financial systems or expertise it had promised, it didn't have the cash flow needed to fund its growth, and there were numerous conflicts of interest between his partners company and the one his partner owned with Dash. In addition, the contractual relationship with the carrier was with Dash's partner's company, not the one Dash owned 50 percent of—leaving Dash in a very weak position. And then when Dash realized it would take legal action to make his situation right, he learned that it wasn't about justice, it was about the interpretation of the wording of their shareholders agreement and the credibility of witness statements.

Says Dash, "I would never sign an agreement again where I was being held hostage like that. If one partner's responsibility is the financial statements, I'd be sure to structure an agreement that specified that the books would be done in house, not at a remote location controlled by someone else. You need to have access to accurate, unbiased, up-to-date financial information and control over who produces it.

"It was probably one of the most stressful things I've gone through in my life. Your whole livelihood, your whole future, is on the line. You've invested all this money in this thing, and you're either going to walk away with nothing, be in the hole, or possibly get what you feel is actually yours. The problem is that you feel very righteous, because you're the person that's been ripped off, but that doesn't mean anything. It's not about justice; it's about interpretation."

CAUGHT BETWEEN A ROCK
AND A HARD PLACE

Factsheet

Name:	Peter Davies
Title:	Junior Partner
Company:	Harrison Zulver
Type of Business:	Marketing and graphic design
Location:	London, England
Annual Revenue:	1.75 million (GBP)
Employees:	35
Years in Business:	Not disclosed
The Edge:	Stuck between two warring partners, entrepreneur faced personal liability for their actions.

The Story

Before starting The Creative Consortium Ltd., Peter Davies was a junior partner in a design and marketing company. The firm grew to 35 employees, with annual revenues of about 1.75 million pounds (about $2.5 million). But when one of the partners started another company, the problems began.

Says Davies, "John set up another company to take on this new line of business that he was developing. But it began to cause ripples with Andrew and me, the two other partners. We felt that we should either have part of the new company, or we should reevaluate the share value of the existing company. Or at least we should talk about it. John was using our resources to set up this new company—our secretaries, our telephone system, our back office. I was quite young, but Andrew finally said, 'Enough is enough. We all want to know what's going on.'

"While this was happening, there was a decline in our overall business because of the recession. So we were kind of stuck. While we should have been rallying together, supporting each other, and finding our way through this problem, our senior partner was concentrating a lot of his time on another business. Eventually, Andrew decided to leave and took a lot of his own clients with him. John, the senior partner, was very upset and said, 'I'm coming up near retirement, and you guys should be looking after me. I've helped build the company, and it's payback time.'

"After Andrew left, John became quite bitter and decided that we hadn't agreed that Andrew could leave. In fact, he wanted Andrew to pay the company the trading value of the clients that Andrew had taken, and that's when it all began to get rather messy. John proceeded to sue Andrew for leaving the partnership and, as a participating partner, I was caught in the middle. If Andrew lost and couldn't pay, I felt I could be brought in as a third-party concern in the partnership. In a bizarre way, I was the one suing and being sued because I was still in the partnership. It was bloody crazy.

"John personally entered an individual voluntary arrangement—it's like a bankruptcy, a reorganization of your finances—because he was so much in debt with this other venture of his; he was just in debt all over the place. This meant that he could get free legal aid, and he had unlimited resources to go after someone, which he used to go after Andrew. This forced Andrew to get a good lawyer to defend his corner. And the ripple effect of that meant that I had to do the same. And I kept saying to John, 'Look, I'm incurring costs here because you're suing Andrew, and I'm being dragged into it.' And he said, 'Of course I won't sue you,' and I said, 'Well, put that in writing, then.' And when he wouldn't, I said, 'Well, in that case, I can't support you *or* Andrew.'

"Over a number of years, this thing just sort of unfolded, and the court kept on saying, 'Look, this is ridiculous. You three partners go away and sort it out among yourselves.' But, John had unlimited resources and was very bitter, so he just carried on, accusing Andrew of leaving the partnership too early, taking the clients, and causing the decline of the business. Meanwhile, Andrew was coming to meetings with tape recorders under his belt and producing transcripts in court.

"It kept on going until it got to the high courts, and we all had to employ barristers and all the rest of it. When we got there, we found that John's prosecutor couldn't make it that day and had sent along another chap. This fellow seemed very unprepared about how to present the case and, after two hours of speaking, the judge asked him 'Are you suing Peter Davies or not? Very simple question.' And the bloke looked and said, 'Well, no, no, we're not really.' And the judge asked, 'So why is Peter Davies sitting here in court, and why is Peter Davies having to defend this case for three and a half years? Case dismissed against Peter Davies.' So within about five minutes, I was allowed to go, and won my side of things. And Andrew won his case the next day.

"After that, I decided, 'Never again will I go into a partnership.'"

Lessons Learned

Many people enter into partnerships without really understanding the long-term ramifications to themselves and to the business of doing so. As Peter Davies learned the hard way, entrepreneurs need a lot more knowledge and guidance about the laws governing partnerships, how to choose and deal with lawyers, when to seek counsel from a lawyer, and how to weigh business issues against legal issues when they have to make tough decisions. Lawyers need to be involved in many aspects of the business—for example, incorporation and choosing the right legal structure, partnership/shareholder agreements, intellectual property protection, client contracts, key employee contracts, processes for firing people, IPO or sale of the company. You should also discuss the legal aspects of a partnership with an attorney, before you begin entering into a legal relationship. Entrepreneurs who barrel ahead without getting good counsel do so at their peril.

Says Peter Davies, "A lot of people like someone, or they get excited about an idea and say, "Let's go into partnership and set this up." I don't think they really understand what they're getting themselves into. There are laws that define your liability as a partner in a company. I'm amazed that so many people in a partnership don't know the laws that govern a partnership. They should—for their own protection."

GETTING CONNED

Factsheet

Name:	Mike Meek
Title:	CEO
Company:	Intellitec
Type of Business:	ISO consulting
Location:	Bucyrus, Kansas
Annual Revenue:	$3.7 million
Employees:	29
Years in Business:	Not disclosed
The Edge:	Partner falsified credentials, caused personal loss and embarrassment, forced company to rename.

The Story

Mike Meek started a company right out of school. Says Meek, "After a year and a half, I took on a partner. It was one of the best and the worst things to ever happen to me. It was the best thing because I surrounded myself with professional businesspeople. We ended up with a staff of 12 people at one point. I would have never been able to do that had I not gone into the partnership. It helped catapult me to a much higher level.

"It was also the worst thing because I lost a significant amount of money in that partnership—and ultimately I determined that

my partner was a con man. I don't say that lightly. He claimed that
he had two Ph.Ds from different schools. After things started not
adding up, we actually checked into it, and the guy didn't even
have one Ph.D. As soon as I found out that what he had repre-
sented as truth was false, I ended the relationship. I told him I
would not be in business with him any longer, and we actually
closed the company down.

"He had racked up a lot of debt, and I was young and stupid. For
instance, he didn't have good credit, so I had signed for his cars,
using my good name. He was threatening to claim bankruptcy on
his personal stuff. But I said, 'That's not the way I work, and that's
not the type of person I am. If my name's on it, it's going to get
paid.' So I took all the debt, anything that had my name on it, and I
told him, 'If you walk away now, and you leave the business to me,
I will pay off all these debts. You go along with my rules, or else these
things are going to be a problem.' So he walked away, and I covered
all those loans. I grew up in a town of 1,800 people, a small town. I
trusted everybody. This was my first real experience that people will
lie to you, and that was a big deal to me.

"I was so upset that I changed the name of the company. Then I
grew that business to a point where we were doing very well. I again
took on a partner, but this time I was a little smarter. I took on a
minority partner. I really liked the guy a lot. We set some goals and
agreed that within 18 months he would produce $2 million worth of
revenue. He produced $30,000. At the end of 18 months, I ended
that partnership. That was a tough one because there was nothing
negative between us, like there had been with my previous partner.
It was simply a performance issue. And I've since started several
more companies—the last one with a great partner."

Lessons Learned

When it comes to partnerships, Mike Meek did everything wrong
when he took on his first partner. He took on a partner without
thoroughly checking out his resume or his references, he signed

for his partner's car loans despite the man's poor credit history, and he incurred a lot of personal debt and reputation damage when his partner turned out to be a charlatan. Even though Meek was able to get his partner to leave the company, he felt he had to close the company and do a re-start because so much damage had been done. After two negative experiences, Mike Meek thought he would never enter into a partnership again—but he has.

"I swore I would never be in another partnership after the first two. But with my new electrical contracting company, I am in a 50/50 partnership. At the end of the day, if it's the right person, then a partnership is okay. But I would still advise against it for most of the people.

"Formal partnership agreements are very important. That's what enabled me to get out of my last partnership, the one where I had to fire the guy. I got the lawyers involved up front and we talked about 'What if this happens? What if that happens? How will it be handled?' ahead of time. So it was all clearly defined in the partnership agreement.

"The advice I'd give other entrepreneurs—because I've lived it and experienced it—is to ask all the tough questions up front. I don't care how much you love somebody, ask the questions up front. Sit down with your partner and go through all of the conversation. What if? Divorces? Breakups? Then make the lawyers put the contracts in place very quickly."

ALWAYS KNOW WHERE THE EXITS ARE

Factsheet

Name:	Greg Ferguson
Title:	Partner
Company:	Triton Real Estate
Type of Business:	Real estate development
Location:	Raleigh, North Carolina
Annual Revenue:	$4 million
Employees:	5
Years in Business:	Company founded 1997
The Edge:	Incompatible values, lifestyles, and plans for the company forced partners to break up the company.

The Story

Soon after Greg Ferguson left his career as a naval aviator, he landed a job with a national consulting firm in Raleigh, North Carolina. He discovered, however, that the amount of travel he was required to do in pursuit of his work was incompatible with his family's needs. With a background in real estate development and entrepreneurship, Ferguson moved in that direction. While cold-calling prospects in the Raleigh area, he met an established developer who was in over his head with a number of projects and desperately needed help. The two became partners and started Triton Real

Estate. It wasn't long, however, before their differing business philosophies began to create tension between the partners.

"His father was a wealthy guy in a small town, and he was kind of the country club type. When I hooked up with him, he had gotten into a couple of deals that I thought had some merit. At that time I thought we had complementary skills. I had the logical thinking skills and a systems perspective. I had been in consulting firms with a couple of hundred clients and had seen what people were doing right, and what they were doing wrong. I don't want to say our partnership was a disaster from the beginning because we did an awful lot of good work together. We put together some terrific office systems, a terrific network with investors and banks, and we built ourselves up to a significant-size company. But the things that I thought at first were complementary—like two star-crossed lovers who think the other's differences are kind of cute and quirky—ended up becoming problems as we got farther down the road.

"He brought an outside-the-box thinking that I didn't have at that time. Since then, I think I have significantly expanded my ability to do outside-the-box thinking. He could look at a real estate deal and try to see it from a number of different angles and possibilities and make offers and make suggestions, and see it in a bunch of different ways.

"Soon after we hooked up, we brought in two more guys, so we had a partnership of four. My strength is on the front end—finding the land, putting the deal together, and putting all the pieces in place. The other guys' strengths were following through on that. And that's the role that my original partner was supposed to have when we joined up. But he began looking at deals that we had no interest in—deals in Charleston, and a marina in Florida. A number of these deals were just way, way out of bounds, at least for our line of thinking. Wake County here is a growing metropolis like Atlanta was 20 years ago, so why was he looking at stuff 300–400 miles away? We have so much opportunity right here that there is no need to extend our risk by going so far away.

"He got us involved in a project in Charleston that was flawed from the beginning. I should have—we all should have—recognized it. I ended up writing a check to walk away from the deal rather than give it back to the bank. At first we put up with his behavior, but when it started costing me hard dollars, that wasn't acceptable. Not only that, but in the meantime, he looked at a number of deals on the side on his own and lost a lot of money. He'd go spend $50,000 on engineering and planning and then figure out that the deal wasn't worth it. He used to spend money wildly, which is way, way different from how I grew up—kind of from the wrong side of the tracks.

"At first, we thought we were going to be able to control the damage and put him in a corner and say, 'Why don't you just do your deals, and we'll do our deals?' But he didn't like that solution. He thought he was the reason our company had accomplished anything, and I took offense at that. The third partner saw all the flaws and saw all the problems. But the fourth partner was on the fence. If the three of us were on one side, it would be easy enough to say, 'See you later.' But the fourth guy was less inclined to want to do that. He saw some intangibles that were important to him, like the location of the office. It was hard to get him to make a decision one way or the other.

"So, we're dividing up the business and I'm setting up a new company in separate office space. It's going to be an amicable separation. We know that we are on very different wavelengths."

Lessons Learned

When entering any partnership—no matter how long you've been friends with your partner-to-be, or how well you think you know him or her—it's in your interest to have a written partnership agreement with clear provisions for the dissolution of the partnership. If you don't have a good partnership agreement with the exit provisions spelled out—for example, what happens to the company name, offices, trademarks, intellectual property, equity, equipment, clients, and so forth in the event of a split up—then you're out of luck.

You'll find that your only recourse, like Greg Ferguson's, is to leave and start all over again.

Says Ferguson, "I look back on this and say, 'Would I have done that again?' and I would have to say that the answer is probably 'Yes' because I had an opportunity to learn an awful lot.

"At first, it seemed like it would be a huge embarrassment, but you see it in the paper every day, people breaking off and starting new companies. I now think of it as more of an opportunity—new image, new logo—than a liability. I did it once. I can do it again.

"Some people build up a company with employees; others build it with partners. If you go the partner route, it's just as important to have a clear definition of what the partners' roles are and what they are going to be responsible for as it is if you have employees. There has to be a distinct role for everybody to play, no matter what kind of company you have, or it can lead to trouble."

SELLING YOURSELF SHORT

Factsheet

Name:	Tina Holden
Title:	President
Company:	Absolutely Wireless, Inc.
Type of Business:	Wireless telecommunications services
Location:	Altamonte Springs, Florida
Annual Revenue:	Approximately $1 million
Employees:	3
Years in Business:	Company founded 1996
The Edge:	Owner gave away part of company with little in return; lost control of company.

The Story

Tina Holden started her company as an exclusive AT&T wireless telephone dealership. Not content to handle only AT&T products, Holden became one of the first traditional dealers in her market to go nonexclusive by bringing in other product lines, including Nextel, Verizon, and Sprint. It didn't take her long to realize, however, that she had given up far too much ownership of her company for far too little capital, and that she was the one doing all the work.

Says Holden, "I had sold some phones to a friend of mine, and he approached me to get into business. He gave me $30,000, and I gave up 50 percent ownership of company to him. I had the client base. I did the legwork. I did everything. I was the only one operating the company. And I look back, and say, 'Oh my God. I sold myself out.' And I soon learned every lesson you could possibly learn about what not to do.

"I had a great marketing plan, but I had no business plan. And I chose a partner who didn't want to invest any time in the company.

"In the beginning, I felt like I was the luckiest entrepreneur in the world because I had this experienced entrepreneur as a partner who had invested in my company. But it was a game to him. He was banking on it going well, and he didn't do anything to support me. If he had been smart, he would have said, 'Hey, let's give her somebody to run the operation and let her go out and bring in all the deals. Let's back her up.' But that's not what he did.

"He manipulated me a little bit more until I gave up controlling interest of the company. I thought we were going to bring in somebody to help me run the company, but my partner decided to pull the rug right out from underneath my feet. One day, he started withholding my paychecks; before long, I was owed a lot of money. I had invested all my savings and everything in my business, and for the first six months of our existence, I worked for nothing. He ended up backstabbing me in the end. Finally, I decided to leave the company and do it all over again.

"Thirty days later, I had a new business. I bootstrapped it, took a $2,500 certificate of deposit and borrowed against it, and I had a couple of MasterCards and Visas; one of my vendors—AT&T Wireless—allowed me to have 30 days' credit before paying. I brought in a bunch of activations that I was going to be paid for 45 days later. That money—about $12,000—is what I used to bootstrap my new start-up.

"Everything was going great, so I decided to hire someone to run the operations. I paid him $36,000 a year, but he didn't do the job. I ended up having to do his job and mine, too. By that time, I was sinking every dollar I could get my hands on into the company and just barely making the minimum amount of money myself.

"I could have claimed bankruptcy, but I didn't want to go that route. I downsized my operations, sold like crazy, paid all the bills, and got the business down to the bare-bones minimum. Things began to turn around again. I did a 200-phone deal down in Miami, won top agent of the month, and I was on a roll again. The company's about $1 million in annual sales, and we're growing. Life is good."

Lessons Learned

Tina Holden was not the only entrepreneur in this book to be edged out by a partner who put in money but nothing else. The same thing happened to Scott Corlett when he founded NextGift. Scott has started and run four companies, including the gift manufacturing and distribution company where he faced similar partner issues. Inexperienced, trusting, and naïve, they were so anxious for money that they let someone they didn't know well buy into their company and get majority control of the stock. The partner then claimed there was not enough money to pay the entrepreneur, took over control of the company, and the entrepreneur was forced out. The fact that Tina, Scott, and the others pulled themselves together, moved on, and started other companies is commendable. But the bottom line is this: If you don't choose a good partner and don't have good legal protection, someone else ends up profiting from your investment of time, energy, and money.

Looking back, Tina Holden now realizes the precarious position in which she put her herself—and her business—when she brought in a partner and took his money without understanding what that meant. She says, "If you don't fully understand the impact a partner will have on you and your business, don't do it and don't take outside money.

"There are times when I honestly say I don't want to do it alone anymore. I would really like to find someone to be a part of the business who wants to do this with me. But if you have a partner or somebody on your board or in your company who doesn't share your values, you're going to have real problems. I learned a big lesson: Be sure that anyone who is going to share a business with you also shares your values."

≈ Wrap-up ≈

The message you should take away from these stories is not that partnerships don't work, therefore don't do them. Partnerships are just like marriages; some of them work, some don't. But the long-term success of a partnership depends first on picking the right partner, then developing the partnership to be more than the sum of each partner's contributions. Finally, success is related to anticipating problems and therefore having good legal documents in place that protect each partner—and the company—from performance problems, reputation problems, death, and disposition of the assets during the dissolution of the partnership.

Here are some lessons to remember:

First, don't jump into the partnership because you're in a hurry to "get going." Be patient. Get to know your potential partner from a business perspective as well as a personal perspective before entering into a partnership. Check out the person, get references, do some due diligence, work together, and make sure that his or her skills and resources are what you need to grow the company. And make sure you share similar values.

Second, have those tough discussions, the "what if this happens" discussions. What happens if his or her performance does not meet expectations? What happens if one of you has a life-threatening disease, should die unexpectedly, or simply wants out of the partnership? Who gets what if you have to close the company?

What about your differences in management styles and approaches to problem solving? These conversations will reveal a lot about the person and whether he or she is the kind of person you want to partner with. Listen closely to see whether you and your potential partner share the same goals, agree on the culture you want to build, and can work with each other without butting heads.

Third, remember that it takes a lot of work to develop a partnership that is more than the sum of the partners. A partnership, like a good marriage, depends on open communication and sharing; it requires compromises, routine checkups, maintenance, and even repair. Set up regular times to talk with your partner, and discuss important decisions. Once a year schedule a partnership meeting and review the state of your partnership as well as the state of the company. Bill Payne, an entrepreneur and angel investor, has founded or assisted in the founding of many companies. In his first company, his partner was older than he was and wanted to exit before Bill was ready. Bill's advice is this: "You have to talk about the possibility that one partner may want out early. Before that happens, you have to start thinking and planning about how you're going to finance the exit of that partner, and how you're going to manage the transition."

In the next section you'll read the stories of another set of entrepreneurs who have experienced a different set of lessons from the edge. Their edge was related to money.

Top Ten Lessons in Partnerships

1. Know your partner. Screen your partners with more scrutiny than you would a job applicant.

2. Match your values and goals carefully. Incompatibility at the beginning of a partnership is likely to get worse over time.

3. Be prepared for market shifts. If your partnership isn't flexible enough to respond to changes in the market, you may need to go your separate ways.

4. Have an exit strategy from the beginning. Know how you can get out of a partnership. And be prepared to exit if partners start taking sides or if you have conflicting values. Don't be afraid to dissolve it if things go poorly.

5. Understand the partnership laws before you sign a partnership agreement. Know your liabilities and responsibilities, as well as your rights.

6. Minimize your personal risk as much as you can. Partnerships are intended to balance personal investments of time and money, not create personal risks.

7. Know the difference between an investor and a partner.

8. Insist that solid, credible, audited information be shared among the partners. Agree to discuss financials, strategic plans and other critical issues with your partners frequently.

9. Carefully define the roles and responsibilities of the partners and revisit this on a yearly basis.

10. Whatever you do, get it in writing.

≈ Money ≈

Section-at-a-Glance

Overview

Individual Profiles

Profile: Sanjay Parekh
The Edge: Avoided the cash crunch and wave of contraction and failure during the dot-com contraction.

Profile: Niv Ben-Haim
The Edge: Entrepreneur started a second company with his father; almost lost both companies because of poor planning and overextension.

Profile: Tim Riley
The Edge: Long-term decisions without short-term solutions, an overaggressive start-up plan, and a high burn rate almost put him out of business.

Profile: Robert Kulhawy
The Edge: Last-minute reversal by lender derailed expansion plan; sunk costs from expansion eroded profitability and hurt chances for new financing.

Profile: Lance Stendal
The Edge: Biggest customer went bankrupt, leaving a quarter million dollars in receivables.

Profile: Michael Beirne
The Edge: Was forced out of company by venture capital partners.

Profile: Kirsten Knight
The Edge: Changed the business model and expanded the infrastructure just as the market crashed. Had to personally get back in the business, lay off people, and reinvent the company.

Profile: David Schulhof
The Edge: Accounting manager became best friend to everyone, so no one believed he was embezzling; almost shut down company and vendors.

Profile: Bill Kimberlin
The Edge: Assistant embezzled a six-figure sum, with an equal sum owed in past due payables.

Profile: Greg Levin
The Edge: Customer goes bankrupt, bank calls loan, supplier goes out of business, and entrepreneur suffers both personally and financially.

Profile: Derek Harp
The Edge: Company's high burn rate almost forced him to take less than ideal financing, which could cost him control of the company.

Wrap-up

Top Ten Lessons in Money

≈ Money ≈
Overview

Why do so many entrepreneurs seem to be focused on money? Because they need a lot of it to achieve their dream. Unfortunately, too few entrepreneurs know who to approach for different sources of funds, when to do it, or what each source is looking for when it reviews the business plan and the balance sheet.

The first thing to understand is that there are three basic ways to finance growth:

1. Self-financing. If you manage your income and expenses and generate profits, you can reinvest those profits in the business and not have to take any money from outsiders.

2. Debt financing. You negotiate a loan with interest from a bank, an individual, or perhaps from a customer. You are required to pay interest and repay the principal at some point in time. Deferred payments to vendors are another form of debt financing.

3. Equity. Employees, wealthy individuals (angels), venture capitalists, or corporations provide money in exchange for partial ownership (shares) in your company. They will expect to sell those shares for a high multiple of what they paid, usually in a relatively short timeframe (3–5 years).

Government grants, e.g., Small Business Innovation Research (SBIR) grants, are sometimes used to finance growth, but these are often quasi-contracts for products/services rather than grants for the development of your company.

In the beginning, you work long hours. You bootstrap and use your own money to get the company going. You tap into savings, borrow against credit cards, use your house as collateral for your first line of credit at the bank, and may even dip into your retirement funds. Sometimes you can convince your parents, relatives, and friends to provide long-term loans or buy equity in the company. If the company begins to grow, you may approach angel investors for equity financing or long-term loans at somewhat higher interest rates than the bank charges. Finally, if your company has incredible growth potential and needs an infusion of capital to "hit the window" of opportunity, you may be a candidate for venture capital financing. But remember that fewer than 5 percent of all companies receive venture capital, and a much smaller percentage of those ever go public. Before you seek venture capital financing, read on. As Michael Bierne found out, venture capital is "a dangerous servant and a fearsome master."

Having more money is not the answer to the problem if (1) it's the wrong kind of money from the wrong source, (2) you haven't built a company with systems in place to monitor the cash flow and to flag slow cash collection or cost overruns, (3) you haven't used the money to hire the right people, or (4) the environment changes quickly and you're left high and dry.

In the stories that follow, you'll read about a number of entrepreneurs who have learned these lessons—and more. While insufficient capitalization is often cited as a key reason for business failure, poor financial management leads to the same end.

Doug Mellinger (whom we met in section 1) learned a lot about operational growth issues and money with his last company. Even though he was on the cover of *Inc.* magazine and dubbed "the next Bill Gates" he had to learn many tough lessons about growth and financial management. (See section 1 on Leadership for the full story.)

Growth for growth's sake is just not as important as profitability and sustainable growth. The Inc. 500 makes entrepreneurs think in terms of percentage growth. We were on the Inc. 500 list for several years before we went public—hit #42. But you can't keep growing at that rate forever. You really need to understand the step functions of growth and develop your infrastructure accordingly.

For instance, we were growing fast, had multiple locations, and each one started to build its own systems. So we ended up having three or four different accounting systems, and I was getting horrendous data. We needed one company-wide system. The data were detailed enough, but didn't tell me what was going on in the company. For instance, some of the reports were based on the sales momentum that had been built up in the past—but I got no reports on what we were doing now that would ensure our sales success in the future.

This problem came back to haunt them when Mellinger's company went public and missed two quarters' projections.

While some of our stories from the edge are related to poor management, some disasters occur when the entrepreneur does not understand the rules of the game regarding debt or equity financing. Some occur because of hiring mistakes, and others occur when macro-changes have an unanticipated impact on a particular company. All our CEOs found their businesses were incredibly sensitive to the ups and the downs of the market, and they were surprised at how quickly the economy changed—with little advance notice. More than a few were flush with cash one day and facing big deficits the next.

Almost every company needs debt financing to help smooth out cash flow. You need access to cash to continue in business while waiting for customers to pay for products or services. Almost every company needs to set up a line of credit at the bank. Banks are quite willing to lend money so you can buy land, buildings, or equipment because those are considered "assets" and can serve as collateral. If you default on the loan, the bank has something it can take back, re-sell, and recover most, if not all, of the money loaned to you.

Banks can also provide a line of credit to help smooth out cash flow, but first the entrepreneur must be willing to pledge personal assets—house, a certificate of deposit (CD), or some other collateral to guarantee the loan. Eventually the bank may lend against the company's outstanding receivables, if the borrower has proven to be a good customer. Once in a while, a bank may even provide a loan to buy another company that has enough assets to collateralize the loan.

But banks and bankers always try to minimize risk. They are lending other people's money, they have an obligation to protect that money, and they do not want the publicity that comes with taking someone's home because the person defaulted on a bank loan. For these reasons, banks are sometimes known as "fair weather" friends: there when you don't need them, and not there when you do. Contrary to what a lot of entrepreneurs may think, banks are not in business to fund company growth. They are in the business to lend money and minimize risk. And the minute your company looks like it is having financial problems, the banker perceives increased risk.

Some of our entrepreneurs found that just when they needed more financing, the bank pulled their line of credit and demanded repayment of money they had borrowed against the old line of credit. If you have developed a good relationship with your banker and you are a good customer with lots of integrity, the bank may give you a little slack while you work out your financial issues. Be sure to build a relationship with your bankers when you don't need the money. Meet with them, discuss your business plan, show them your cash flow and balance sheet. Set up a line of credit as soon as feasible. Draw down on it and then repay it to demonstrate that you are responsible and that you have the capacity to repay. Check in with your banker now and then, report on how the business is doing, and develop a relationship that is strong enough to carry you through a financial crunch.

Greg Levin, president and CEO of Perfect Curve, Inc., faced personal and business disaster when a customer went bankrupt at the end of the year, left him holding a $100,000 receivable, which created a loss for the year and broke his loan covenants with the bank. When it came time to renew the line of credit with the bank, Greg told the banker what happened and what they were doing about the problem.

> We had a meeting with our banker in March, and we told him what we needed. Our banker said that everything was great, 'I just need one signature. You guys are doing a good job. You'll get through this.'

Although the banker appeared to be supportive during the meeting, the bank was not. Not only did the bank not renew Greg's quarter-million-dollar line of credit; it asked him to repay the outstanding loan as soon as possible.

Even when you have built a good banking relationship, things can go wrong. If your bank officer moves on or there's a new boss who begins to second-guess your bank officer's recommendations, your bank gets sold to another bank, or the bank's board of directors decides that the bank should change its percentage of loans in various categories, you can get caught—and some of our entrepreneurs did. Robert Kulhawy's business was in high growth mode until his banker pulled the rug out from under his financing plans and reneged on the promise of a bank loan at the last minute. The impact was devastating.

While banks and other debt financing sources can cause problems, other sources of money can be equally problematic. Angels often "bet" on the entrepreneur to achieve the dream, and they look for CEOs who are coachable. But they may become too engaged in the company, may begin to meddle and try to get the entrepreneur to manage "their way." And while good venture capitalists provide financial and knowledge capital in exchange for equity in the company, remember that venture capitalists are solely interested in the potential of the company, not the entrepreneur. Their investment is in the company, and in some cases they figure the entrepreneur is a liability; hence they require the entrepreneur to step aside as a condition of investment. They will not hesitate to replace the entrepreneur, the CEO, or the management team; sell the company; or even close it down if it does not perform as promised when the deal was struck. Michael Beirne found this out the hard way.

And financing growth by selling shares to the public through an initial public offering is a path that's also fraught with danger. If you think banks or venture capitalists put restrictions on your company in exchange for the cash you need to run it, you're in for a really nasty surprise when you go public. Capital obtained through public offerings has lots of legal and financial strings attached. And if you miss your quarterly estimates of earnings, your stock—and you—will start down a slippery slide. The changes that result from going public are major. Sam Boyer, co-founder of Brothers Coffee (who is featured in section 2, on People) commented:

> Going public made it harder for me to implement changes in the company, and it required quite a few new processes that didn't add to our bottom line or increase customer satisfaction with our product. It slowed down the business, and it had a negative impact on communication within the company.

What happens if you raise money and expand in an up market, and the market turns south? Angels and venture capitalists will try to re-price at a lower valuation. Banks may pull the loans, and customers may disappear. As some of our entrepreneurs found out when they had over-expanded, when the bubble burst, they were left on the edge, with a dramatic decrease in revenue to support their company. Kirsten Knight, president and CEO of the Seattle-based staffing agency Creative Assets, Inc., built out several new locations in anticipation of continued rapid growth fueled by her technology firm clients. When her clients went away, she was stuck holding a very expensive bag. Says Knight:

> I opened the two new markets in Atlanta and Austin. These were big investments; we built them out for success. Then the market changed. A lot of our clients were in technology, and some were dot-coms themselves. The market started

slowly evaporating from April to October, and then from October on, it just disappeared. We haven't made money in several months.

Kirsten Knight is one of many entrepreneurs who found they had a burn rate they couldn't support and had to make massive changes. But they didn't just retrench, they reinvented their companies.

Finally, one lesson our entrepreneurs learned about money is to raise more than you need and spend less than you have. Few entrepreneurs had enough funds to take full advantage of the market opportunity, but even if they did, their rapid, uncontrolled growth, poor planning, and inexperience led them to spend more than they had. In hindsight, all of them see what they did wrong and would do it differently if they could do it again. They shared their stories so others could learn from their mistakes.

As you read the stories that follow, consider your company's need for money and think about how you can avoid the predicaments these entrepreneurs faced. Think hard about your answers to these questions:

- Do you know the difference between building a business and building a company?

- What makes your business model work? What are your drivers? How do you make money? What happens when one of the drivers changes?

- Do your financial systems provide the information you need soon enough to make the necessary corrections before you run off the edge?

- Are you tracking cash flow and profits? Revenues and expenses?

- Have you taken the time to build a good relationship with your banker?

- When you are trying to do a significant deal, do you get multiple sources of financing or do you tend to rely on a single source?

- Is your company a good prospect for venture financing? If so, do you know which venture capital companies to approach and what each one will be looking for? Are they more interested in your technology, your customer base, or your management team?

- Are you prepared to be pushed out, have your company sold, or watch it get shot if your investors don't think it can deliver what was promised when they invested?

- How committed are you to the people who helped you build the business? Would you take back your company, even if it created a financial liability for you, to try and save their jobs?

- Does your company have a business plan? Is your plan just a pro forma one to satisfy investors or is it an evolving road map for your business? Has your top team contributed to it? Has your entire company been briefed on it? How often do you refer to it?

Individual Profiles

SURVIVING THE DOT-COM EXPLOSION

Factsheet

Name:	Sanjay Parekh
Title:	Chief Strategy Officer
Company:	Digital Envoy, Inc.
Type of Business:	Software developer
Location:	Atlanta, Georgia
Annual Revenue:	Under $10 million
Employees:	35
Years in Business:	Company founded 1999
The Edge:	Avoided the cash crunch and wave of contraction and failure during the dot-com contraction.

The Story

In the heady days of the dot-com bubble, it seemed that all it took was an "e-" in front of your company name, and investors would flock from miles around to hand over their money. Unfortunately, not every e-business was built to last. In fact, the vast majority weren't. Some Internet entrepreneurs were different, however, and built their businesses on a firm foundation of good planning, cost containment, quality products, and customer value.

One survivor of the ups and the downs of the dot-com era is Digital Envoy, Inc., led by its founder, now chief strategy officer, Sanjay Parekh. Digital Envoy didn't survive because of dumb luck; it survived because of the company leader's commitment to planning. Says Parekh, "Planning is very important to us."

Parekh founded his company to solve a problem he had experienced. "One night I was surfing the Web and I hit two Web sites: the FedEx site and the IKEA site. Both of them ask you what country you're in before you can get to the home page. It's annoying as hell. FedEx makes you choose from 216 countries, IKEA from 33. So I thought to myself, 'There's got to be a better way.' That night I started thinking about the problem and came up with a solution. Our firm received patents on its technology and began to sell its products to other companies, eventually landing some very high-profile clients such as CNN and AOL."

Digital Envoy's technology served a unique niche to online retailers and other customer-centered sites. Their technology could help other e-businesses identify their customer location, thereby improving marketing, demographics, and customer service efforts.

But as the dot-com meltdown began to occur, there was a very real fear that the company might get caught in the downdraft of business contractions and failures. "One of my greatest fears is to hire people and then have to lay them off," says Parekh. "A lot of our fellow companies here in the Internet world have done just that—made massive layoffs. That tells me they didn't plan well enough ahead. They didn't figure out what the need was going to be in the long run, so they over-hired or overextended. I don't want to ever have to lay somebody off because of my stupidity. I'll fire people if they're not doing the job. That's their fault. But if I haven't planned well, then that's my fault and somebody else shouldn't be the victim of that. I've tried to be very careful and thoughtful about what we do and to make sure we don't waste anything in terms of people, money, or equipment."

To ensure that the company would not have to resort to layoffs Parekh had to do extensive financial planning and develop strategies for securing financing and making it last. Says Parekh, "At the end of 1999, we started raising money. It was a private round of money—angel funding, about $1.5 million. We made the money last because we are intentionally frugal. Early on we realized we needed some exposure out west to gain the interest of the venture capitalists (VCs), and so we developed a plan to do that. We did this through Garage.com. Those folks were very helpful in getting our name out and getting introductions and meetings set up. In the fall of 2000 we were one of three companies selected to present at one of their showcase events—right there in the Silicon Valley to about 200 local angels and VCs. We got some good leads from that.

"When we started the company, our plan was to make money one day, but it wouldn't be through eyeballs and advertising type of stuff. We came up with a service that was valuable to people, a business model where we could make money. We charge all of our customers a monthly subscription fee. So as customers get locked in, it just adds to our revenue base. At the beginning of 2000 we were one person—me. We did a tenfold increase between 2000 and 2001—and now we're about 35.

Lessons Learned

It takes a very strong leader to run a lean organization when all of your colleagues and competitors are spending money like it's going out of style, as was happening at the height of the dot-com frenzy. While everyone else was burning through venture capital like there was no tomorrow, Sanjay methodically developed austere financial plans, stuck to them, and avoided the cash crunch that doomed so many technology companies when capital dried up.

Parekh said, "Right now we're flush with cash. We're still not spending anywhere near what other companies like us are spending. We're still very conservative in terms of spending money. Our employees understand that, and they say 'I think I've got a secure future here. So let me make sure I help out and not waste money or spend money on frivolous things.'

"A lot of our success is a direct result of planning, but I won't say that all of our success was intentional. Some of it was by accident, but a lot of it was planning, because that's the way we are as people."

Parekh advises fellow CEOs to plan and not to overspend. "Don't spend on silly things. We've seen companies buying expensive cars and furniture, advertising on billboards and doing expensive Super Bowl ads. You've got to be sure that you can afford to spend $2 million for a 30-second ad, and you've got to be sure that you can quantify that this expenditure is going to get you more than $2 million back in terms of value. One of the problems that caused the dot-com meltdown is that people didn't run the numbers to see whether spending on things like Super Bowl ads would bring more than $2 million in value back to the company. An Amazon.com needs to drive consumer awareness and a $2 million Super Bowl ad might make sense. But in a company like ours, it doesn't matter if consumers know about us or not. Consumers are not our market."

By planning, controlling costs, and spending only on things that added value to the company, Parekh was able to keep his company from going over the edge, unlike many of his competitors.

WHEN GOOD MONEY CHASES BAD

Factsheet

Name:	Niv Ben-Haim
Title:	President
Company:	D. Enterprises
Type of Business:	Promotional Products Printing
Location:	Toronto, Canada
Annual Revenue:	not disclosed
Employees:	not disclosed
Years in Business:	not disclosed
The Edge:	Entrepreneur started a second company with his father, almost lost both companies because of poor planning and overextension.

The Story

Niv Ben-Haim and his brother started a promotional product company that focused on corporate logos. One day a friend at a golf tournament asked if he knew of any Canadian company doing promotional mouse pads. After three weeks of research and development, Ben-Haim started making them, and eventually became the one-stop shop for mouse pads in Canada. The company doubled, then really started to grow. When his father and a disgruntled friend decided they wanted to leave the company where they were working and start a company making vinyl products, Ben-Haim decided the two companies should move in together and share a larger facility.

"I was 26 at the time without a lot of business experience. Being young and aggressive and believing in myself, I decided that no matter what, my father and his friend should open up a business. I felt obligated to help because it was my dad, he wasn't in good health, and he hated working at the other place. A few years before that, my parents had opened a business that had gone bust. So I knew first-hand what it was for somebody to have a business failure.

"We were underfinanced, we had no business plan, we had done no planning at all—we were flying by the seat of our pants. We never sat down with a lawyer or an accountant, never got advice about how to proceed. We wanted so much to make this a business that we ignored everything that logic tells you to do. And guess what: We ran out of money in three months.

"The mouse pad business was generating income, but that was being eaten by the vinyl business. And it got worse. Finally, a friend who happened to be a client sat down with me, did some projections, and showed me the only way to get through this was to borrow $150,000. We were facing a recession in Canada, the business was not going the way we figured it would, and now I had to go to the bank and personally sign for a $150,000 loan.

"We didn't want to do this, and the bank didn't really want to give us the money. I had to fight for it. How close to the edge was I? I was in a basement apartment with my wife and two kids, starting my own business. When I made a commitment to help my dad, it took me backward two or three years. I feel that I wasn't making any progress at all. At one point I almost hoped that their former employer would sue my dad and his friend and close them down for competing against them. That was a real low point.

"Fortunately after we got the loan, things turned around. I have a business that's going well, and my dad and his partner are now drawing salaries from their business."

Lessons Learned

Ben-Haim learned firsthand why it's important to plan, do some financial projections, and develop "what if" scenarios. "I've learned that putting together a business requires careful planning. Do your homework and involve people in areas where you have no expertise to help you think it through and warn you about things that could happen. And make sure you have a reasonable business model."

Another lesson he learned was this: "Don't take money from a profitable business and pump it into a losing proposition without having some limits, some checkpoints. And the minute it approaches those limits or looks as if it's getting out of control—in terms of the amount of money it requires or the amount of time it takes away from your main business—stop and reassess the situation. You may decide to continue, but make that a conscious decision; don't keep going deeper into the hole."

Ben-Haim is one of several entrepreneurs who advise that you periodically reassess whether the original business model is still valid. Another example is Jim Anderson. Jim had a computer training company that boomed, then crashed. He decided one of his biggest lessons was to "make sure you look at your business model very closely. I knew that we were only doing a break-even model, but I didn't realize that no matter how much I grew, I was never going to do better than break even. Our customers were not willing to pay us what we needed to get paid to be profitable. And if we couldn't come up with a reason for them to pay enough for us to be profitable, then we should have shut down the business a lot sooner. I made a big mistake. I should have looked at the business more objectively as an investor. I owned it, and I should have asked, 'Is this a good investment or not?' It's my life and my money. If it's not a good investment, I shouldn't be doing it."

Howard Getson (profiled in section 2 on People) was co-owner of a software company and found that prevailing technology played a bigger role than he had anticipated in the success or failure of his company. "We had some of the best and brightest people. We were 'thought leaders,' and we were very proud of the advantage our software gave our customers. What we didn't realize was that the best technology wasn't as important as the most prevalent technology. As we watched Microsoft and Lotus fight it out, we saw the fear, uncertainty, and doubt grow in our marketplace, and we realized that better technology was irrelevant. What mattered was having the technology that the greatest number of people were willing to invest in. We were lucky to get sold to a public company, but I got back only what I had invested in the company. Now I look back and realize I got more than I would be getting if we tried to sell it now. That was a tough lesson to learn."

Niv Ben Haim, Jim Anderson, Howard Getson, and many other entrepreneurs profiled in this book have learned the importance of planning and understanding what drives your business model. They suggest that you periodically reassess your business model and make sure it will be profitable. They also advise that you track technology developments, economic changes, currency variations, and other macro-changes in the external environment that will impact your customers—and your business.

MAKING THE RIGHT MOVES

Factsheet

Name:	Tim Riley
Title:	Founder and Board Member
Company:	Door to Door Storage
Type of Business:	Moving and storage
Location:	Seattle, Washington
Annual Revenue:	$10 million
Employees:	210
Years in Business:	Company founded 1996
The Edge:	Long-term decisions without short-term solutions, an overaggressive start-up plan, and a high burn rate almost put him out of business.

The Story

While working for a large, traditional storage company, Tim Riley was bitten by the entrepreneurial bug. He sat down and wrote a business plan for a new business, tore it up, wrote another business plan, tore that up, and then finally decided on the concept of Door to Door Storage. With Door to Door, the company drops large moving containers off at a client's house. The client fills them at his or her leisure, and then Door to Door picks up the containers and delivers them wherever the client wants them to go. But, as with any new approach to an old problem, it took time—and more money than expected—to prove that the concept was an economically viable one.

According to Riley, "We lost a lot of money while we were trying to figure out the business model. Five months after we started our business, the largest competitor in the mini-storage business got into the business and did a rapid rollout of the concept. They moved into 55 locations within 12 months. Everybody thought we were roadkill—but they never proved the unit economics. So they rolled out 55 flawed models that were very expensive to fix. The company I used to work for also jumped into the market, and they stubbed their toe badly in the business.

"Capital is a big barrier in our business because, unlike unit storage where you've got a big real estate asset you can use as collateral for financing, our business is purely a service. The bank says, 'Well, Tim, if I give you five million dollars, what assets will that money buy?' And I say 'Your money is going to pay for a bunch of wooden boxes.' And they say, 'Well, we can't lend against that.' We looked for venture capital, but we were competing for capital in the technology era of 1998, 1999, and 2000 when investors had obscene concepts about what rates of return should be for an equity investment. If they couldn't double their money and be liquid in a week, they didn't want to talk to you. They kept saying, 'Why can't you be like Webvan?' Well, today, we look like heroes. Webvan is long gone, and we just did a very large equity financing—tens of millions of dollars of equity financing in the worst venture capital market in recent memory.

"But everything didn't always go smoothly. In the first 12 months of our business, we had $5 million in the bank but we were losing $300,000 a month. The board had no tolerance for losses, and they pulled no punches. I would come out of board meetings in tears, not because board members were being brutal or unfair— they were just being honest about pointing out the obvious shortcomings in our business. But these were people I had respect for, and I wanted them to think highly of me and my abilities. I hadn't yet figured out a solution to our problems; it was very frustrating, and the answers were not magically appearing overnight.

"Today, we're trying to pull off an aggressive expansion. We're tied to some fairly restrictive performance milestones, and we have a board of directors that's very wary of increasing fixed costs in the business. So, how do you pull off a rapid rollout without spending the money to put a huge infrastructure into place? Everybody's working 18-hour days, and we are trying to be very efficient with our time. We're in midst of this right now—we're trying to pull it off. We're lean and mean. I believe we are going to make it, but if we lose just one player, we're at risk. We're number 54 on the Inc. 500 list this year. We'll probably drop into the 100's next year, and then probably be in the top 20 the year after that."

Lessons Learned

Rolling out the expansion of a business—like Tim Riley's Door to Door Storage—takes a lot of money. There are warehouses to rent or build, trucks and other equipment to acquire, people to hire, supplies to purchase, advertising to place; a substantial investment must be made before the first customer pays for the service. In proving the concept for Door to Door, Riley admits that he made a lot of mistakes and burned up a lot of money in the process. Here are Riley's lessons learned.

"You've got to understand the key drivers of your business and make sure that you have the right competency within your organization to (1) identify the business drivers and then (2) optimize them. We've done a lot of measuring and management of key business drivers, and we make them very visible. I assessed my strengths and weaknesses, and I recognized that one of my weaknesses was analyzing our profit and loss, so I hired a chief financial officer (CFO) right away and made sure that I had high-level analytic ability in the company.

"Another thing I learned was not to underprice our services but to learn how to sell value. If you call around San Diego and check the rates, you'll find that we're not the cheapest in town. But if you ask who's going to make you happy at the end of the day, it's going to be us. There are about 43 different things that can and do go wrong with our competitors—and I know, because we hear about them every day from people who come in and tell us, 'We made an appointment with so-and-so. They were ten bucks cheaper, but they never showed up.' So don't try to compete with the big boys on price; sell value.

"Make sure you set goals for both revenues and profitability. I give my managers bonuses for making revenue targets as well as bottom-line targets—but they've got to hit them both to get the bonus.

"Finally, when you are in start-up, keep your costs and commitments short term and variable. Don't sign anything long term in the first 36 months or so of your business. Try to keep everything as short term as possible because you don't know your business well enough to know what's going to go right and what's going to go wrong. In my case, we leased way too much warehouse space in Los Angeles when we set up operations there, and that contributed to the $300,000 a month burn rate that almost put me under. I made the mistake of signing a five-year deal on three times more space than I needed. So when I didn't use the extra space, I had to go out and sublease it, pay a commission to the agent who subleased it, and it was a nightmare. So be sure to limit your long-term liabilities."

DIVERSIFY YOUR FINANCING

Factsheet

Name:	Robert Kulhawy
Title:	President & CEO
Company:	HFI Hardwood Flooring, Inc.
Type of Business:	Floor covering products
Location:	Calgary, Alberta
Annual Revenue:	$30 million plus
Employees:	85
Years in Business:	Company founded 1981, Sold 2001
The Edge:	Last-minute reversal by lender derailed expansion plan, sunk costs from expansion, eroded profitability, and hurt chances for new financing.

The Story

Nick's Flooring Service Ltd. was originally a small, family owned floor covering installation and service company, which grossed about $700,000 in the late '70s. Robert Kulhawy joined the family firm in 1977, eventually becoming president and CEO.

In 1981, seeing the market need, Robert founded a wholesale hardwood flooring division. During the '80s and '90s, Kulhawy developed a strategy for growth, and the company grew to $20 million in revenue. Seeing the opportunity for an industry consolidation and exponential growth, Robert then brought in a partner and took the company public, and then undertook a rollout strategy that resulted in even more rapid expansion. The company completed two acquisitions and, by spring 2000, had several more lined up that would have a dramatic impact on company growth. Unfortunately, there was a change in plans.

Says Kulhawy, "By late spring of 2000, we were in effect operating a $100 million business, including the deals we had lined up that we hadn't closed yet. We were focused on a final funding transaction for a particularly large deal that would take place on Friday at 9:00 A.M. However, that Wednesday afternoon our bank advised that they couldn't fund at the agreed level. To say we were shocked would be a gross understatement. It was a really, really good company we were acquiring. The assets were excellent, and this was going to be an asset-based lending deal. We were buying under market. It just didn't make any sense at all why the bank would wait until the very, very end to let us know there was going to be a problem. You hear about this kind of thing happening to other people, but you never in the world think it's going to happen to you.

"It was Wednesday at 3:00 P.M., and we had to have the cash in their hands by Thursday so the deal could fund on Friday morning. We got caught—we couldn't raise the additional money because we only had a few hours to get this mess straightened out. Later I found out what had happened. Technology stocks had just died and the stock market had plunged. Even though we weren't a technology company, we got caught up in the crash. We couldn't get an extension, and we just really cratered. We ended up with an infrastructure set up to run this $100 million-plus business, and overnight our revenues were a third of that.

"And then our bank—which had pulled out at that last minute—started to change the rules on us. They started constricting our cash, so we suddenly had less cash available. Since the amount of inventory they were lending on was dropping dramatically, that started to squeeze us.

"So we very quickly developed a reorganization plan that included an informal proposal to our creditors and said, 'We're getting some trouble here from the bank. Why don't we stretch out your payments for a period of time? We'll still get you 100 percent of your funds owing plus interest.' But we couldn't get everybody to sign onto this 'informal' proposal. And meanwhile, we had a bank that wasn't being very cooperative.

"We eventually found out that the reason was that our bank— which was U.S. based—had made the decision to basically get out of Canada. We simply got caught up in a decision somebody made in another part of the continent. So we sold the main operating business and the business lives on with a different owner. We paid out the bank. Our attorneys and reorganization consultants said that when a bank pulled out like that, they had never seen anyone keep their company out of a receivership or bankruptcy. But we managed to have enough assets to pay the bank out, and to pay certain obligations.

"We're currently in the process of building a manufacturing business. I honestly believe that we can have a much bigger and much more profitable business than we had before. We're certainly headed in that direction. We have the technology. We have revenues. We have the plans in place and we're moving through the process. In the next three or four years, I really expect the business to be in the $70 to $100 million revenue range—and much more profitable because we're selling technology that has a far higher margin. We think it will be a much more valuable entity than we would have had before."

Lessons Learned

No matter how good your banking or other financial relationships are, there is always a chance that some outside event, something beyond your control, some decision made by someone you don't know, could turn a relationship squarely on its head. When the technology stocks took a dive in 2000, many financial institutions pulled back from some of their "riskier" investments. In the case of HFI Hardwood Flooring, Inc., this translated to "investments in

Canadian firms," no matter how solid the businesses or the relationships. Regardless of where your business is located, and with whom you do your banking, it's always a good idea to have two or more financial institutions involved when you are trying to close a critical deal. Don't put all your eggs in one basket. Divide the deal into several pieces, or have a backup financing in place in the event that your primary funding source evaporates.

Robert Kulhawy learned this lesson the hard way. "I said for years, never put all your eggs in one banking basket. But I did, even though I knew better. I should have had a couple of other banks with different pieces of the deal. I should have been more demanding, but I had one bank that was really gung ho—saying all the right things—until the day they changed their policy. That really came back to haunt us."

As a result of his tribulations, Robert Kulhawy's faith, family and personal well-being took on a much greater priority in his life. "I've gotten far closer to God over these couple of years. I've had much success in business, and expect to have more in the future, but never again will I ever put at risk, the most important things in my life—my faith, my family, and my health—to achieve it."

Jeff Dennis's grandfather may sum it up best, "Believe in one God, but make sure you have two bankers!"

PUTTING ALL YOUR EGGS
IN ONE BASKET

Factsheet

Name:	Lance Stendal
Title:	President
Company:	FuturePages, LLC
Type of Business:	Media planning and placement
Location:	St. Paul, Minnesota
Annual Revenue:	not disclosed
Employees:	not disclosed
Years in Business:	not disclosed
The Edge:	Biggest customer went bankrupt, leaving a quarter million dollars in receivables.

The Story

FuturePages began putting small businesses on their Web site, much like a Yellow Pages directory on the Web. When founder Lance Stendal decided to change the business model, he brought in a business partner and began to shift the company's strategy. Over time, FuturePages evolved into a media planning and placement firm, specializing in college newspapers. But when a key customer went bankrupt, he realized that he needed to reexamine a lot of FuturePages' financial practices.

Says Stendal, "We had a large client—a dot-com that was on the verge of going public. But instead of filing an IPO, the company filed for bankruptcy and left us holding close to $250,000 in receivables. This happened more than a year ago, and we're still working it through. When we sensed that there was a problem, we started talking with our vendors, the publications we work with, to let them know what was happening. We were very up front about it.

"We've had to turn to factoring (a form of financing based on selling accounts receivable at a discount to a third party). That has been the only thing that's gotten us through. But it's really expensive money. We've also had to raise some additional funds from existing investors to help with cash flow. And we've become a lot stricter about our credit requirements. We now require more of our customers to prepay; and this has helped. Finally, we've become more selective in who we work with.

"This has been very tough on me personally. You feel bad about not being able to take care of your vendors and that's been very, very difficult. It certainly is stressful when you've got them hounding you for payment and you're trying to work through these arrangements, especially when you're dealing with 125 vendors. But I feel a commitment to these people to work through this thing, to get it squared away and to keep the business going. I think we have shouldered our share of the burden of responsibility to the vendors and to the shareholders, who are mostly friends and family. You certainly don't want to walk away from either of those two groups."

Lessons Learned

Although it's tempting—and easier—to have fewer rather than more customers, be careful. Placing the future of your business in the hands of one or two large customers can put you on the road to disaster. When Lance Stendal's biggest client went bankrupt and stiffed him to the tune of a quarter of a million dollars, he quickly realized his company was in the danger zone and that he needed to put systems in place to prevent this from happening again.

Says Stendal, "Just because a company says it has the money and promises to pay doesn't mean a thing. We've become much, much more diligent on our credit analysis of potential customers. This experience has taught us to be much more careful in managing cash flow, so we're very aggressive in collections. And it's taught us a lot about managing vendor relationships.

"We've also learned that the legal system can be used against you, even when you go in thinking that you've got a pretty solid case. We've had some problems in getting this thing resolved—and we're not going to receive anywhere near the amount of money we are owed. And that has taught us to be very specific in our proposals and contracts and to develop a solid paper trail.

"We now monitor sales volume on a weekly basis. For us, that's the real big number. We watch that number very closely because if it's okay, everything else will fall into place. I'm always looking at where we are right now. And we've got most everything set up on a schedule. We've got enough of a cushion, especially with working with a factoring company, so if we need some money to cover us for a week, we can tap into it pretty easily and that helps us to get over those peaks and valleys.

"But my final lesson learned is not to let the company become too reliant on a single customer. We'll never again put all of our financial eggs in one basket."

ON THE OUTSIDE LOOKING IN

Factsheet

Name:	Michael Beirne
Title:	Founder
Company:	Infomech Internet Commerce; Novaforge Total Security
Type of Business:	Software, Technology, Security
Location:	McLean, Virginia
Annual Revenues:	$3 million
Peak Employees:	50
Years in Business:	Company founded 1997
The Edge:	Forced out of company by venture capital partners.

The Story

The company that Michael Beirne founded in 1997—Infomech, an e-commerce professional services and training firm—was profitable from day one and growth was driven by sales. In three years, Infomech quickly ramped up to more than 50 employees and over $3 million in revenue with approximately 30 percent going to the bottom line. They were picked as a Deloitte & Touche Fast 50 company.

The company remained profitable through the dot-com implosion, and Beirne subsequently led a $4 million-plus fundraising round to turn the company's homegrown yet successful e-commerce solution into a leading software contender. However, Beirne was quickly ousted from the company, over a disagreement on sales strategy and management. Within a year of the founder's ousting, the company had closed no new sales, had burned though cash, and had gone right over the cliff, filing for bankruptcy within 18 months. What happened to cause this dramatic change? Michael Beirne took venture capital without fully understanding the VC game: specifically how the differing goals of founders and venture capitalists can derail a company.

Says Beirne, "We were getting some awards and recognition and most importantly we were growing sales and investing all profits into a next generation release of our product. That's about the time we began getting wooed by venture capital. They liked that we had remained profitable, were weathering the dot-com storm (although dot-coms were about a third of our customer base), and that we had a product with some traction. I raised a round of $3.5 million for about a fourth of the company. I had a minority partner, but my ownership was more than two-thirds of the company before the VCs, and over half the company after they came in."

"The VCs brought up the idea of bringing in an experienced management team, and I embraced it—along with an additional chunk of money to accomplish this task. We brought in a president to run the day-to-day operations who had been a senior sales VP at a software company that had gone public, and I thought this would help bring the company up to the next level. We also brought on several folks from his management team, and I expected sales to skyrocket with all these experienced hands. But the opposite happened—things began to rapidly change for the worse.

"Within weeks after raising the money, sales softened dramatically and all of a sudden I had internal political opposition to some of my sales prospects. I had lined up several deals that were below our projected software sale price but were still profitable. Each of those deals was sidelined by the VCs and the management team the VCs had encouraged me to bring aboard. Why? The rationale went something like this: Taking those deals would have changed our business model from the one we presented in the fundraising round—and that would substantially lengthen the time to reach the higher valuation the VCs needed to be able to exit within their 18–24 month timeline.

"Unfortunately, this did not become clear to me until after I had agreed to extend our funding round to deal with sluggish sales and the cost of bringing on an 'experienced management team.' This brought my share of the company just below 50 percent, yet between my partner and me, we still had over 50 percent control. I never expected my partner to shift sides, yet he did. Within nine months of my ousting, he had become president of the company. The company burned through cash, while losing customers—a very painful thing to watch from the sidelines. In hindsight, I should have realized this could happen and either retained control or ensured that any 'experienced management' I brought on could first prove their capability with results. It quickly became clear that having experience running sales for a company with a proven product does not necessarily prepare a person to lead a company or sell a fledgling product."

Lessons Learned

When Michael Beirne lost his company, he learned a very hard lesson: that bringing in venture capitalists to provide financing for your company can be a disaster if you don't understand the conflicting interests between a founder and the venture capitalists. Never is this difference more apparent or painful than when the company hits a rough spot.

"While it can be embarrassing to recount such a disastrous failure on my first venture capital experience, now that I've been through this, I learned a lot and I hope other entrepreneurs can learn from and avoid my mistakes. I've met several other entrepreneurs who've had experiences with venture capitalists eerily similar to mine. When things go bad and you are in a fight with your VC, things can go from bad to worse fast—from hiring away your management team for their other investments, to direct intimidation, legal saber rattling, political wrangling, and more. Once you lose control, it is a slippery slope and difficult to get back and set things right.

"Another lesson I learned is that whenever you bring in outside money, you run the risk of corrupting the lean and mean efficiency of a bootstrapped startup and changing the culture that brought you so much success. If you are not careful, more money can turn into higher costs, which can then turn into even more costs. This can screw up your priorities and put the company into a death spiral that is tough to pull out of.

"Money by itself doesn't solve anything. Sales do. Customers do. Consistent alignment of values and goals do. Squeezing every bit of value out of a dollar, getting concrete measurable returns from every investment in the company—from a phone system to a marketing campaign—never loses its importance.

"Unfortunately, the additional money from the venture capitalists allowed our team to feel less urgency about what had made us a successful small company: namely, nailing down every single customer we could and making them happy. The new management brought on support staff, conducted 'marketing studies,' and other non-revenue generating activities like rebranding the company, which in hindsight was utterly ridiculous. We could have been successful if we had stuck to our original focus and values, which had made us successful: making more profits by operating more efficiently, and developing better solutions for an expanding customer base.

"I'd say there has to be a clear, concrete reason for taking money from venture capitalists, and if you are going to do it, be sure to have your own counsel—do *not* use the company's lawyers, as they will not ensure your best interests are covered and they may not warn you of all investment risks. If you are going to take on money from an investor, get as much as you can in the first round— bridge financing and down rounds only throw gas on the fire if the company gets into trouble. After funding, be just as frugal and be sure to invest only in projects that lead to clearly measurable returns, and manage the company so you can quickly retrench and take a defensive position if the market tells you it is time to weather a storm. Live to fight another day!

"I've learned that most venture capitalists are not willing or interested in doing whatever is necessary to make your company a success. While some VC firms are great catalysts and help good ideas and small companies become great businesses, a lot of VC firms are focused more on their short term return on investment (ROI), instead of the long term success of the company.

"Don't forget that VCs need to be able to show book value to their own investors as they go. If you aren't hitting your numbers, they won't hesitate to interfere with your sales strategy, tactics, and results; or to replace you—in order to achieve the results they want. Venture capitalists' goals are not always congruent with what might be in the best interests of a company, not to mention the founder(s). If you are going to raise money, be sure to talk to several entrepreneurs who have had good and bad experiences—before you approach an investor or take a dime."

SWIMMING AGAINST THE CURRENT

Factsheet

Name:	Kirsten Knight
Title:	President & CEO
Company:	Creative Assets, Inc.
Type of Business:	Staffing agency
Location:	Seattle, Washington
Annual Revenue:	$10 million
Employees:	20
Years in Business:	Company founded 1990
The Edge:	Changed the business model and expanded the infrastructure just as the market crashed. Had to personally get back in the business, lay off people, and reinvent the company.

The Story

Creative Assets, Inc., is a staffing agency that specializes in the placement of high-end, creative professionals, including commercial designers or copywriters, project managers, and producers. Kirsten Knight started her business in 1990—just before the tech company explosion that created a huge market for creative professionals. Sales grew quickly by 20 to 50 percent a year. When you're in a strong-growth market, it's easy to believe that you always will be. But, as Kirsten soon learned, what goes up eventually must come down.

"Late last year I really expanded my plans by moving into Atlanta and Austin, and had plans to move into Boston, New York, and D.C. In preparation, I ramped up my staff and the company operations. I brought in a president who was a pretty high-level executive with the largest staffing company in the world—paid big fees, relocated her, the whole thing. I brought in a high-level marketing person. I had everything wrapped up and ready to go.

"I opened the two new offices in Atlanta and Austin. These were big investments; we built them out for success. Then the market changed. A lot of our clients were in technology, if not dot-coms themselves. Our market started slowly evaporating from April to October last year and then from October on it just about disappeared. I increased my expenses at the very moment the market evaporated. Our sales, year to year, were down 50 percent and our expenses were up about 50 percent. I had always tried to be smart, and I had never stuck my neck out on the block that much—but the one time I did, I just got whacked. We haven't made money for several months.

"It's been incredibly stressful. I've had to set limits and say, 'I'm going to give it until this date, and if the picture doesn't change, this office is shutting down, and that office is shutting down, and this person is gone, and that person is gone.' And those are tough decisions because it's like trying to decide when to sell a falling stock. You have so much invested, and you tell yourself, 'If I close it or sell now, I'm going to kill my upside of ever making this money back.' I had set limits in the past, but those decisions were about where to invest, what new markets to go into, and how many new people I should I bring on. Those decisions are a lot easier than when I had to close offices and lay off people. Over and over I found myself thinking, 'I really value these people, but I just can't afford them anymore.'

"I wish that I had already had a recession or a downturn under my belt, because I needed some experience about how to handle this. We're currently in Seattle, Portland, Denver, San Francisco, and Los Angeles. We had almost 60 employees last December. Now we have 20. Last year, revenues were $29 million. This year they'll be about $10 million.

"Fortunately, there's a bit of light at the end of the tunnel now. I just had a better month than I was expecting. Not that sales were great, but we lost only 20 percent of what I was expecting to lose. I think by this fall, depending on what happens, we should be doing a lot better, which is great. But I realize it could be a month-to-month kind of deal for the next year, depending on what happens to the economy. I'm thinking that the way to increase revenues may be to consolidate and cut costs. I guess I'll have to give up an ownership percentage and control and so forth, but I'll do what I have to do to survive."

Lessons Learned

While Kirsten Knight could not have anticipated the extent of the economic recession, she put her company at risk by expanding her infrastructure before she had the clients and contracts to support her new offices. By tying up so much of her cash in infrastructure to support future growth—leasing office space, hiring company officers and staff, and more—she had very little flexibility to respond quickly when the bottom started to fall out of her market. If she had made these infrastructure investments more slowly, or shared the risks with partners or other companies, she might not have taken as big a hit to the bottom line.

Says Knight, "In the future, I'll operate differently, because I've been through this downturn and I know now how quickly things can change. In good times I'll probably store up a lot more reserves. Someone once said to me, 'Run your company as if 70 percent of your resources were suddenly taken away.' I am going to remember that, no matter how good things are. You know, when I look back, it's amazing the amount of money that was spent on unnecessary things.

"Another lesson I learned is that the more successful the business became, the less confident I became. I felt that I had gotten lucky because of the economy, and I kept thinking, 'I don't really deserve this. I don't think I have the skills to do this.' But this year, I've had to get in there and roll up my sleeves, take over the reins, make these decisions, and have the hard conversations. I am not a perfect leader by any stretch of the imagination, but I'm honest and I think I lead sincerely. This year I earned respect by doing what I have to do. And it's given me confidence. When it really came down to it, I made the decisions, I kept fighting, and I got back up after being knocked down."

"HE OFFERED TO LEND ME MY MONEY"

Factsheet

Name:	David Schulhof
Title:	Managing Partner
Company:	Envisions
Type of Business:	Computer products
Location:	Burlingame, California
Annual Revenue:	over $5 million
Employees:	15
Years in Business:	Company founded 1989
The Edge:	Accounting manager became best friend to everyone, so no one believed he was embezzling; almost shut down company and vendors.

The Story

David Schulhof is a serial entrepreneur, having started four different companies. His second company—Envisions—was a direct marketing company that sold computer products, specifically scanning products and imaging equipment. After coming off a reasonable success with his first company, Schulhof was ready for a new challenge. Once he got past the typical ups and downs that every new business goes through, things started looking good—until his accounting manager drained the company's bank account.

"My first accounting manager decided to leave, and I had just started the recruiting process when I got a call from an employment agency. The agency wanted to know if I needed an assistant. I said, 'No, I'm really happy with my assistant, but I do need an accounting manager.' They told me that they had an accounting manager available. I'd never used an employment service before, but I figured it would make my life a little easier. They indicated that the candidate was a very good person, and they sent him over.

"I met with him, and he seemed okay. I had one of my board members who had an accounting background meet with him, too. At this point in my business career, I paid very little attention to operations and accounting. They were more of a nuisance to me than anything else. I was focused on sales and marketing and business development—the things I thought really mattered. Well, I quickly learned that other things matter, too!

"He seemed very polished and able to do the job. I didn't really look at many other candidates. The employment agency was selling me hard on this guy, saying how lucky I'd be to get him and that I should hurry up and snag him because he had multiple offers. This was the first time I'd dealt with an agency, and I figured they're not going to send me a criminal, so I didn't do any of the background checks I normally do when I hire someone new. Big mistake!

"So this fellow joined my company. I paid the agency thousands of dollars for the honor of sending me this fellow. I had a company of 15 to 18 people at this point, and he quickly made friends with everybody. Before long, everyone thought he was a great guy. He took people out to lunch all the time, and he was a very sociable guy. He was buying his co-workers gifts, and buying gifts for their children. What I didn't know was that he was buying all these gifts with my company's money.

"He didn't do all that well as an accounting manager. As a matter of fact, the accounting reports and the reports I needed to run the business got more and more confused. At the same time this was going on, my business was growing by leaps and bounds, 50 or 60 percent each quarter. I was pretty happy because money seemed to be pouring in. But then vendors started calling me saying that they weren't getting paid. Since my business was rocking and rolling, I thought I should have had a ton of money in the bank, and I couldn't understand it.

"After a month, I still didn't have any financial reports, and things were getting crazy. My accounting manager claimed there were problems with the software we were using and he couldn't get support. He claimed that the bank statements hadn't come in from the bank or that they were lost. In the end, I just thought he was not very competent, and I let him go.

"Then I started going through things. I found checks he had written to himself, which he had endorsed and put into his account—which was at the same bank I dealt with. He would go to my bank, obtain some counter checks, and sign them to himself. Normally, I signed all our checks. But my accounting manager forged a signature card that allowed him to sign checks all by himself. I wasn't even aware of it.

"We had two accounts: one with a bank in San Jose, and another one in Burlingame. He never visited the San Jose bank, but he routinely wired money out of it. The bank didn't have my authorization that would allow him to wire money, but somehow he was able to do it anyway. When I started seeing these checks and the money transfers, things got very surreal, and that's when I went to the police. I told them I had all these checks and I'd like them to go arrest this fellow. They were a little bewildered because the evidence was so out in the open. It turned out that the only thing that he didn't do was cover his tracks—at all. They had a hard time believing that somebody would do this and be so blatant about it. But I'd been in business for years in that community, I was credible, and I had very compelling evidence. They put an investigator on it, and he eventually apprehended my ex-manager at his house with cars and rugs, paintings and furniture, expensive clothing and jewelry, and all the other stuff he bought with the couple hundred thousand dollars he had embezzled from me.

"Towards the end, before I fired him, he actually offered to lend me money. How outrageous—to offer to lend me money he had stolen from me! He stole $200,000 from me. He didn't do it with a gun. It was worse than that. He befriended his co-workers and then, by stealing money, put their jobs at risk. While he was telling everyone what a great guy he was, he was jeopardizing a whole lot of jobs, not to mention the risks to our creditors, investors, and me. We dealt with a lot of small companies. We were a big customer to many small companies, and we would have put them out of business if we hadn't paid our bills. It took about a year, but we finally paid off everybody.

"After I discovered all these problems, I had to figure out what to say to my employees. I couldn't say, 'This guy just embezzled money from us and I don't know what's going to happen to the company—whether we'll make it or not.' I had to keep pretending that everything was normal and try to keep the company together. I didn't want people looking for jobs. We needed everybody to be working. When I had stabilized things and had a plan, I brought everybody together in an all-company meeting. I told them that some money had been stolen, but that we had replaced the money, the company was secure, and there was no need for them to worry. But I wanted them to know that this great guy—this guy you thought was your friend—he stole money from the company. People couldn't believe it, their jaws dropped. I even took my managers to the sentencing to watch him in his orange jumpsuit and handcuffs get marched in front of the judge and get sentenced to two years in San Quentin.

"I learned a lot about our justice system. The average bank robber is considered a blue-collar criminal, gets away with $3,000 per event, and gets five years in jail on average for that. The average white-collar criminal gets away with $50,000 per event and only gets six months in jail. It was my ex-manager's first conviction, so there were limits on the penalty. The maximum penalty for embezzling that amount of money is two years, which is what he got."

Lessons Learned

While some embezzlers may work their trade over a long period of time, taking amounts of money too small to trigger any alarms, other embezzlers do things in a big way. Although Schulhof fired the new manager within three months after he was hired, the manager was still able to embezzle $200,000.

Before this happened, Schulhof didn't pay much attention to the numbers. Now he does. "I learned that you've really got to pay close attention to your accounting processes. That's an area that we entrepreneurs tend to ignore. Now, I get my bank statements mailed to my house so nobody can intercept them. And I make sure that I have checks and balances, that we have one person handling our receivables and a different person handling the payables. I do background checks, no matter where the person comes from. I don't have anybody sign checks except me. If I have to, I can authorize a check verbally for someone else to sign on my behalf.

"I've also learned to ask any serious candidate for their social security number and get their permission to do a background check and credit report on them. I've weeded out people based on that. I've come across people with multiple social security numbers who can't explain it, and then don't show up again after I bring up the question. Bottom line is that I've learned to be much more diligent when I am hiring people into my company."

Dave Schulhof was approached by an employment agency that had a candidate they were "pushing." Paul Hickey, Doug Mellinger, and Chris Rosica talked about headhunters—companies that hunt for people who meet your specifications. Don't be confused by the two. And don't think that using either one can absolve you of your responsibility to do your own due diligence on individuals you are thinking of hiring. If you don't do it yourself, be sure to have someone you trust check references, academic credentials, former jobs, titles, and past performance of prospective employees.

As Paul Hickey said, "It's your money!" so pay attention to the management of it, the flow of money through your company, and the people who are handling the money. The final lesson Chris Rosica learned is that it's not just hiring the right people that counts but getting the right people matched up and in the positions where they can perform well, then tracking performance, learning from the high performers, figuring out why others are not performing as well, and taking appropriate action.

CAUGHT IN THE ACT

Factsheet

Name:	Bill Kimberlin
Title:	President and CEO
Company:	OBJ Marketing Corporation
Type of Business:	Clothing
Location:	Brentwood, Tennessee
Annual Revenue:	$1.5 million
Employees:	10
Years in Business:	Company founded 1991
The Edge:	Assistant embezzled a six-figure sum, with an equal sum owed in past due payables.

The Story

Bill Kimberlin started OBJ Marketing Corporation in his third year of college. The company bought damaged merchandise (mostly jeans) from apparel manufacturers, repaired them, and sold them to outlet stores all over North America and Mexico. Kimberlin was focused on growing the business and entrusted the accounting to his assistant. That turned out to be his first mistake.

Says Kimberlin, "I had an assistant whose primary job was to handle all the receivables and payables and help me with the details of the business. Everything seemed fine, at least until our numbers started going crazy. They were all over the place. So I had my tax attorney come in. We did a surprise audit, but he didn't find anything wrong. Eventually another employee's husband told me that my assistant's husband had been flashing large amounts of cash in a nightclub in downtown Nashville, and things started going from bad to worse. It became clear she was embezzling from me.

"I immediately called my YEO Forum chair and told him I needed an emergency forum. When I got the guy on the phone, I could hardly speak. I was just panicked, and the only words I could get out were, 'My assistant . . . embezzled . . . bankrupt . . .' I was sure I was in big trouble. I just pulled over to the side of road and waited. He called back and about 20 minutes later we had a forum meeting set up for noon. When I got there, there were ten members of my forum at the table, and I told them what I knew. They helped me put together a plan, a process for handling this because I couldn't just go in and say, 'You've been stealing from me and you're fired'; I had to get proof first.

"I started to do a little digging, and it quickly became clear how she was taking money out of my business. When a customer placed an order with my company, my assistant would delete the order from the computer and ship it herself when the check came in. She would then deposit the check from the customer directly into her personal checking account. I couldn't understand how she could deposit a check made payable to my company into her own account. I thought when a check was made payable to someone, you couldn't put it into any other account. But my bank never looked at these kinds of things. She was taking just a little bit at a time, and this went on for about a year. And because we didn't have any inventory management systems, it was very hard to detect.

"But at some point she started getting greedy. She started taking larger checks—$10,000 and $20,000. When I figured out what was going on, I terminated her pending an investigation, started calling my vendors, and that's when I knew I was really in trouble. I found about $150,000 in past-due accounts payables. I figured we had $100,000 in accounts receivable, but because she had taken so much money, there was hardly anything at all.

"Just before I terminated her, she had taken the garbage out to the dumpster. On a hunch, I went out, got in the dumpster, and I started searching through the company's trash. When I started finding statements for the mortgage payment on my house, I knew I had another really big problem. I'd been writing the checks to pay my bills and giving them to my assistant to mail. But she just threw away the statements and deposited my checks into her own account. When creditors called to speak with me, she would screen the calls, so they never got through to me. At that point, I took out a warrant for her arrest.

"I felt pretty much like an idiot because it was my fault that it happened. I wasn't paying attention to what I should have been watching. I was leaving too much and too many details to somebody else who turned out to be dishonest. I learned a lot of lessons from that one.

"She ended up taking about $150,000. I negotiated with all my vendors, enough to keep me in business. I reorganized everything and started the legal process, which was a complete nightmare. The bank where she was taking the checks refused to meet with me; they finally said that if I wanted half my money they would be willing to settle for that. But I knew I couldn't get by with just half of the money she took.

"I thought that when somebody took a check or forged a check, the bank covered the loss. But that turned out not to be the case. So I started conducting an experiment. I signed checks Mickey Mouse, Donald Duck, Harry Brown—all kinds of names, and they were clearing. I signed a $17,000 check with just a squiggle for a signature. Then I took a check for $4,000 made out to XYZ corporation and signed by Bill Clinton, president, and endorsed it Bill Kimberlin. I went to the bank, deposited it into my account and it cleared. At that point I knew I had enough to go public.

"I asked the bank again to meet with me, but they refused, so I went public and a CBS station ended up doing a story that ran all day long, 'If you signed your check Mickey Mouse, do you think your check would clear?' (stay tuned).

The bank still wouldn't meet with me. It was a story of David and Goliath. They were going to bankrupt this small business guy if they could to avoid paying. So I called my attorney and said, 'Tell them I plan to sue them and that I'd like to give them a presentation on what I plan to tell the jury. And make sure one of the senior people from the bank is there so that the decision can be made on the spot.' So they agreed to meet with me.

"I went in and I talked to them for about an hour. I told them what it was like to be an entrepreneur, told them about my first sale, how I drove 200 miles round trip and made $68. I told them how exciting it was to be living my dream of being a college student as well as president of a company. I took them through the whole thing, how she embezzled from the company, how I missed it and the tax attorney missed it, about the sleepless nights after I found all my mortgage payments in the dumpster, how I took out a warrant for my assistant's arrest, and the emotion of not being able to explain what's happening when I try to talk to people because the words just don't come out. And when I got done, the bank attorney sitting there, with her eyes glazed over said, 'That's the most incredible story that I've ever heard.' We started negotiating a settlement right there, and I ended up getting all my money back, plus damages—the next morning.

"The woman who embezzled from me became responsible for paying back the bank. She made one payment and then disappeared. Every year for the past three years, I commit a day or so to trying to find her. I just found out that the authorities found her two weeks ago. She was prosecuted for a financial crime and given an eight-year suspended sentence. She's sitting in jail as we speak, waiting to find out whether they are going to turn her over to the state or she's going to be allowed to pick up where she left off and pay the money back."

Lessons Learned

In this classic case of embezzlement, Bill Kimberlin learned a very painful lesson: Just because you're close to someone or you've known that person for many years, or you trust them implicitly, doesn't mean that they won't try to take advantage of you or try to steal from you. People need money for all kinds of reasons, and sometimes their need for money—or their greed—can override the personal relationship.

Bill Kimberlin learned that he needed to make changes and to put in more financial controls to protect his business. "I used to trust everybody. I still trust people, but I confirm. My second lesson was to know what your weaknesses are and to understand how those can hurt you. My weaknesses were detail and organization. I thought I could completely delegate the financial details to somebody else, with no checks and balances. I learned, however, that there are some aspects of business you should not turn over to someone else.

Jeff Behrens, the President of the Telluride Group, a company specializing in IT outsourcing, had a similar insight: "Understanding cash flow and balance sheets, knowing what banks want, what investors want, and understanding the health of the company is hugely important. I've actually enjoyed learning that stuff. I didn't know it in the beginning. Some entrepreneurs think that's the job of the CFO and that they don't need to be bothered by it. But just as a doctor needs to know how to measure blood pressure, I think the CEO's job is to know what a healthy business looks like from a financial point of view and what an unhealthy one looks like, and the relation between the two. It's the CFO's job to develop that information, but the CEO needs to know how to read the balance sheet, profit and loss, and cash flow—and understand what the numbers mean."

Eron Koss, an entrepreneur who has founded a number of companies, clearly identifies the challenge for entrepreneurs when hiring, managing, and trusting others. "Betrayal is the worst thing that can happen to you. You can't be betrayed by enemies, only by your friends. Only the people you trust can betray you. But you have to trust or you can't get anything done. In spite of the problems I've had, I still trust people—but the paperwork better be in order."

Bill Kimberlin has been through a growth experience: "I'm a much better person for what I went through. I'm thankful for the experience because now I've got a much better idea of my company's finances. Before I wasn't very demanding and I was a very trusting man. Now I'm asking tough questions and I'm verifying things and following through. I'll test my employees in different areas. For example, every so often, I take some of my own inventory out of the warehouse at night to see if anyone tells me, to see if my new inventory control systems pick it up. And I run background checks on everybody that I hire."

When Bill Kimberlin started the company, he just started selling. He had no inventory management control systems, no financial control systems—none of the management systems needed to help manage growth. When his assistant deleted an order from the computer, filled the order from inventory, and deposited the customer's payment into her own checking account, he had no way of knowing this was happening. And when he became suspicious, he asked his tax attorney to look into the situation rather than a professional accountant who might have had more experience spotting embezzlement.

Kimberlin's final advice: "Any business that can afford it should have separate accounts receivable and accounts payable persons and should have them bonded. That way if they go crazy on you, you've got some protection. I didn't have that. My business insurance covered only a very small amount of what my assistant took because it wasn't a loss that I planned for. I needed to have a good inventory management system in place, and I needed to test my people. Without getting overly paranoid about it, you've got to plan for a disaster. Now I just tell my employees that we're going to have an audit every quarter."

GETTING THROWN A CURVE BALL

Factsheet

Name:	Greg Levin
Title:	President/CEO
Company:	Perfect Curve, Inc.
Type of Business:	Baseball cap accessories
Location:	Sudbury, Massachusetts
Annual Revenue:	not disclosed
Employees:	not disclosed
Years in Business:	Company founded 1995
The Edge:	Customer goes bankrupt, bank calls loan, supplier goes out of business, and entrepreneur suffers both personally and financially.

The Story

In 1994, Greg Levin noticed that baseball caps were all manufactured with flat brims. And what do people do, after buying a new baseball cap? Put a curve in the brim—with their hands. Levin thought, "What if I could design something that would automatically put the curve in the brim of a baseball cap while the owner wasn't wearing it?" This something became the Perfect Curve Cap Curver. But when his company took off, Levin soon discovered the dangers of being too dependent on one customer, one bank, and one supplier.

According to Levin, "Thirty percent of our business came from one account, a store chain. They were the 800-pound gorilla in the hat business, and we certainly did not expect them to go bankrupt. But they did and they owed us almost $100,000. We had just come off the fourth quarter, one of our biggest quarters. We had a lot of inventory, packaged in a way that I couldn't resell it very easily to someone else.

"I had an angel investor who had lent me $200,000 to start the business. I was ready to give him his last $30,000 when I got the news—had a dinner planned in January and everything, but I had to nix that. I had to take the $100,000 loss for the year, which destroyed my balance sheet and broke all my covenants with the bank. We expected to be profitable at six figures, but we ended up having a five-figure loss—for the first time ever.

"We had a meeting with our bank in March. We told them what had happened and what we needed. Our banker said that everything was great, 'I just need one signature. You guys are doing a good job. You'll get through this.' But a few weeks later, he sent us a letter saying the bank would not be able to support our business or renew our line of credit.

"It was Mother's Day when we got the letter. We were planning to take my mother and father out to dinner at the Four Seasons and see Jackie Mason in concert. We never thought the bank was going to be a problem. But with the bank wanting us to pay them back and no longer having a line of credit, I became very distraught. I thought we were facing the prospect of losing the business.

"Perfect Curve is a family business in reverse. I, the younger generation, started the business and my father works for it. He works with me, and this is his sole income. He needs that job and wouldn't be able to replicate it anywhere else. And that compounded the stress and anguish I was feeling.

"I spent the next three and a half weeks sleeping on my couch because I could not go to bed. I don't have a TV in my bedroom, and my mind just would not relax. I had to fall asleep in front of a TV in my living room. I was sleeping—for maybe one or two hours a night—in my clothes on the couch for three and a half weeks. I did not even want to go in my bedroom. This was just wreaking havoc on me. I even stopped eating for a bit.

"I knew we had to start raising money. We went back to our initial angel, the one we had almost paid back. He said he would give us the money, but he became a little difficult about it, put some restrictions on salaries—all understandable stuff, but time was running out. We had to get back to the bank with an infusion of capital by the end of July.

"We were only six days away from the drop-dead date when my angel came through with a loan. But we needed long-term debt. We wanted a four-year note, and he wanted a one-year note— which is not long term. So I said two years. He said, 'No, a year and a half.' We went back and forth and eventually we worked it out. He lent me some money, which satisfied the bank.

"And if that wasn't enough already, I suddenly had a supply problem. A lot of my products are made in China and brought over here; the lead times are 100–120 days. I had all the stuff ordered, and we thought everything was fine. But the company that did 80 percent of my production got caught up in a scandal. Last year, they were a $750 million company. Now I learn they are going out of business in a matter of weeks. So here I am: a customer who has stepped up to the plate, I've got hundreds of thousands of dollars of orders, and I don't know if my manufacturer is going to go bankrupt before getting me my products.

"I hit that in-between period where I was trying to get out of a lousy inventory position, and I ended up with no product. I had to back order everything for everybody, something we'd never done in six to seven years. Time was running out. I'd been out of product for eight weeks; that probably cost me $30,000 to $40,000 in sales. We finally got our products and started shipping on time, but I tell you, the hits just keep coming and coming.

"The physical toll, the psychological toll, the emotional toll, the financial toll have been personally devastating. The first thing I had to do was cut my salary almost 50 percent. Last year's five-figure bonuses—gone. Insurance policies, profit sharing—gone. My assistant—gone. My director of sales—gone. We absolutely cut out all the fat and did what we had to do to get healthy so we can be here next year. To make a long story short, it looks like we've done it. We've just started to turn the corner. Right now—today—we've done more business than last year. And if we have the holiday season that we hope, we should pretty much be even with last year, if not ahead."

Lessons Learned

One negative event can put your company on the edge, but Greg Levin had four of them in short order. Levin's business—and Levin himself—faced disaster when his biggest customer went bankrupt before paying the $100,000 it owed. This caused Levin's company to default on the loan covenants with the bank, which in turn caused the bank to ask for repayment of money borrowed, and cancel the company's line of credit. When a major supplier went down the tubes after a high-profile scandal, Levin found himself on the edge once again. Adding to the stress, Levin employed his father who needed this job and was not likely to be able to get a job like this elsewhere.

Says Levin, "One of my lessons learned is that it is never a good practice to have such a large percentage of your business tied up in one account. But then my banker didn't help either. He was certainly not there when I needed him. And he didn't even call me with the bad news; he just stuck a letter in the mail.

"I am now insisting on a better relationship with my banker. I want the banker to show me that he wants my business. Perhaps I'm naïve—everyone says bankers are bankers and you're not going to change them. But I want to work with people I trust. I can't work with someone I don't have confidence in.

"I also learned that I was naïve about balance sheet issues and how the bank looks at your balance sheet. Truth be told, we'd been profitable every year for the last several years, but we did not show that profit because we were using some of the cash to buy out our angel investor. That destroyed my balance sheet, and it came back to bite me. My balance sheet did not represent the strength of my company. What's on paper didn't really tell the whole story, and I did not understand the impact that would have when the bank was deciding whether the company was credit worthy. Now I realize I need a strong balance sheet for banks to like me.

"I also learned the lesson of never burning bridges, especially with my angel. He was crucial. We had negotiated a buyout two and a half years earlier, and I called him every month or so, to give him an update. I paid the loan back two years ahead of schedule. He got over 100 percent on his investment. I figured that if I ever needed him again, I could talk with him and ask for his help. For instance, if I got an order from Wal-Mart for a million bucks, I'd need somebody to help finance that. So I learned the value of having that kind of relationship in place when you need to draw on it in bad times."

Levin learned many valuable lessons about growing and financing his company—and a lot about how to deal with stress. This experience took a huge personal toll on him. "I'm still pretty much of a wreck. I'm just coming out of it. This whole experience put me into therapy and on medication. With the family connection and the responsibility—all that came to bear—and I began to think of the consequences of losing the business. It was an ego blow for me, but I worried much more about my Dad. He doesn't have any retirement, so this is his livelihood. It put me into a deep, deep depression. Now that the business is more on track, I'm beginning to think about new ways we can expand it. I haven't been to the gym since the day I got the word about my customer going bankrupt, but I think I can get back there and do something for myself. I need to start dating and getting out.

"I guess the major lesson I learned is that there's always a way out. You just have to believe and keep working at it."

FEELING THE BURN

Factsheet

Name:	Derek Harp
Title:	CEO
Company:	Logikeep
Type of Business:	Computer security services
Location:	Dublin, Ohio
Annual Revenue:	Approximately $1 million
Employees:	60
Years in Business:	Company founded 1997, sold 2001
The Edge:	Company's high burn rate almost forced him to take less than ideal financing, which could cost him control of the company.

The Story

Derek Harp started Logikeep—a computer security services firm—in 1997 with Mike, a friend from his college days. While active duty Navy officers, they both became interested in security technology, and they soon began surveying the market to see who was offering what and to look for unmet market needs. The two began to spend their off-duty hours putting together a plan for a security consulting firm and recruited other team members. When it came time to leave the Navy and devote their full efforts to the company, Derek had a nasty surprise.

"I had spent about $15,000 from my credit cards and personal loans at that point to start the business. But then we found out that my partner, who had key technical knowledge that I didn't have, was not going to be able to get out of the Navy for another year and a half. So all the sudden it was just me. And a $15,000 debt.

"Venture capital was an alien thing to me. That was not something I was comfortable with. Of course, I had heard rumors and venture capital horror stories. And I also thought that most venture capitalists only wanted to do later-stage funding, which a lot of them do. So I focused on angels or the possibility of incubating LogiKeep inside another company—whatever it took to bring it to life. At this point, all we had was a dummy prototype of the application that a customer would use, written in Delphi. We paid a programmer about $3,000 to write it.

"I had multiple meetings, always looking for angel capital and always looking for a way to bootstrap the next 30 days. At some point, I asked some family members to help. My parents called back about a week later, said they were going to take a credit line out on their house, and asked, 'How much do you think you need to keep this thing alive and get where you need to go?' We agreed to draw down $20,000.

"So I rented out my house in Virginia, packed up everything that was corporate in the trunk of my car, and I drove to Ohio where I had some friends who would work for equity. I was selling the vision and selling equity. That's all I had. And I lived at a couple of these people's homes. Every one of those people during that period either became an employee or a shareholder or both of the company.

"A friend of mine from high school—a civil engineer—was in from Colorado, and he came over to visit. My friend saw my Delphi prototype, and he got real excited. He connected me to a guy, who connected me to his father and to this person and that person. Long story short, I went to New York, and I pitched the business to a very qualified angel. Within two weeks he and another angel agreed to do $1.63 million in funding.

"Before the angels came into the picture, I had given out about 17 percent of the company to investors. This first investment round we gave up 35 percent of the company for $1.63 million. We quickly grew from eight people to 80. We raised $9.1 million in capital—all angel capital. But I was financing a pretty hefty burn rate and learning a lot of lessons—some good ones and some painful ones. Our product development took way too long, but by the summer of 2000, we had a handful of beta customers that were finally paying us—Nationwide Insurance, Cardinal Health. All the while I'm continuing to raise funds; angels are leading to other angels. We started talking to venture capitalists, we were able to raise angel money but at less and less preferential rates.

"We interfaced with 71 venture capital firms, and we presented to about 35 of those. Almost half just said no after looking at the business plan. But 15 to 20 moved farther along, with multiple meetings, multiple phone calls, and due diligence. Meanwhile we're raising more angel capital, we're growing, we're adding people, and we're adding capacity. As I look back now, it's easy to say we overbuilt. I now build companies as big as they must be, not as big as they could be. But the ethic back then was to do it right, bang it out of the park, so I was trying to do that.

"We found ourselves with a high burn rate, with customers starting to come on line, when the market began to change fundamentally. It suddenly became much more difficult to raise money. We'd gone through the venture capital mill, and ended up with a deal that was less than desirable. Two venture capital firms were going to do the deal together, and some of the provisions and things they wanted were really hard to live with. About the time we had that on the table, I got wind that a new company was being formed up by the ex-head of a Big Five security practice. So I called him up and asked him what he was doing. He said, 'I'm in New York, and I'm starting a full service security firm and we are doing acquisitions.' I suggested that we needed to talk. I flew to New York for an hour meeting that became a marathon. We stayed for three days and hammered out a deal. In the end, we decided to take the acquisition over the venture capital deal because of the provisions that none of us were comfortable with.

"Money had definitely become an issue, and I had a premonition. I decided that I wasn't going to push my luck to save my title or my equity. After $9.1 million of outside investment, I still had 40 percent of the company. I knew if I made decisive changes I could avoid the prospects that many companies were facing of complete losses for everyone involved. I felt that the best thing was to be very open-minded and not to be greedy. And sure enough, we hammered out the acquisition after three straight days and came to terms by close of business on Friday. As we gave it one final review, the largest investor and I came to the conclusion that the terms presented some risk to the investors the way it was written. So I offered to make up the difference, coughing up 14 percent more of my personal ownership, making the new numbers work better. My investors accepted the sale, and the deal went through. To this day, I don't regret it."

Lessons Learned

Like many companies of the era, LogiKeep built out its infrastructure long before it had a product to sell. This pattern, once established, became the rule. The result was that Logikeep had a voracious appetite for money, and this required Harp to be constantly searching for new sources of cash to support the company's high burn rate. To keep the company strong, the high burn rate nearly forced Derek Harp to accept a venture capital deal that he felt was "unreasonable." Finally he decided the best route was to be acquired.

Harp says he learned a lot of lessons: "Be burn conscious. Don't spend too much money. You've got to figure out benchmarks and milestones and say 'We're only going to spend so much,' or 'Our burn is only going to get so high—we're just going to have to figure out a way to make do under that burn.' I would first ask 'What is the minimum required to make money?' Not the minimum number of people to make a world-class product, but what's the minimum we need to begin to have customers. You may very well end up with a lesser product for a period of time, but that's okay. I could have sold a less robust product at the end of 1999, instead of waiting until spring of 2000 before I had something to sell. I would have had early revenue. We had a world-class product, best in class—still do today—but we also were running a huge risk. We called it Death Valley, the desert where we weren't making sales but we were still consuming a lot of money.

"And we didn't just grow too big; we grew too fast. Our business plan—the plan I wrote—said that we had to have all these capabilities in place. But we really didn't need to have them all at once.

"I've learned that you should be shrewd about spending capital, both from self-funding and outside sources. You should develop burn projection plans and work very hard to stay at or below those levels, never linking your spending directly to the assumption that you'll realize your ideal revenue projections. Think creatively when you're building new businesses. Both you and your investors will be very thankful in the end."

≈ Wrap-up ≈

Money makes the business world go 'round, but it can also derail a lot of great ideas and good people in the process. Getting control of the financial side of the business is a must in order to avoid the edge.

Tim Riley spent a long time trying to make his business model work. First he had to understand the key drivers of his business, and then figure out how to optimize them. He learned to set both revenue and profitability goals, manage against them, measure his team's performance against them, and made sure that everyone in his organization understood what it would take to make the business model work.

Tim also learned not to under price his offerings but to sell value. Next time he will keep fixed costs to a minimum during start-up and not make any long-term spending commitments for the first 36 months.

Kirsten Knight experienced high growth and built out her infrastructure before she had guaranteed revenue. When the market went south, she was left holding the bag and went from 60 to 20 people, and $29 to $10 million in revenues. But she's learned she can manage growth on less money, a lesson that Michael Beirne and Bob Kirstiuk also learned.

She has also learned is to build up more reserves—financial as well as personal. While she didn't really want to, she climbed back in the ring and fought for her company. She made the hard decisions about cuts, laying off people, and downsizing. Doing so increased her self-esteem and made her ready for future adversity. It wasn't just luck—it was leadership that enabled her to guide her company back from the edge. She understands she may need to reinvent her company to stay competitive, and she's now confident that she can do so.

Robert Kulhawy got hit hard by a decision made elsewhere in the bank. It's little consolation that the bank's policy change was unrelated to his company—or to the value of the deal they were doing. Unfortunately, Robert had counted on this single funding source and had no alternative funding sources in his back pocket. Eventually he recovered, paid off the loans, reinvented the business and now has something even bigger and better. But he has learned that multiple sources of funding helps spread the investment risk, just as diversifying your investments helps spread your personal risk.

Derek Harp planned the optimal company and built it, then found he had to keep raising money to keep it going. Ultimately his choice was to sell the company or accept financing with terms he felt were onerous. He sold. Derek now understands that he grew his company too large, too fast and didn't weed out people soon enough. Next time Derek will ask, "What's the minimal amount of money, people, product I need to get started?" Next time he will hire slow and fire fast.

Michael Beirne went after the most tantalizing source of capital, but he didn't understand the rules of the venture capital game. When a venture firm brought in a new team, renegotiated the deal, scaled back the company, and then fired Michael, he was stunned. Unfortunately, it's a familiar story. Few first time entrepreneurs understand that most venture capital companies expect very high returns on their investments, within a relatively short time frame. If you take venture capital money, you need to know that you will be replaced and/or the company will be sold, most likely within three years. The venture firms are not interested in you—or in the company if it doesn't perform up to expectations. So think carefully about all this before you seek venture funding. Find out whether the goals of the venture firm are congruent with your goals *before* you take their money. After you do the deal, it's too late to turn back; the balance of power will have shifted.

Michael also discovered that the influx of big money changed the start-up culture of the company to that of a "big company." He learned that too much money can actually destroy some of the entrepreneurial spirit.

Looking back, Bob Kirstiuk (profiled in section 1 on Leadership) is amazed at the amount of money they raised and spent and knows he can grow his current company for a lot less money, as well. He, too, has learned that money and stock options aren't always the best motivators. People who received stock options did not automatically think and act like owners. In fact, when stocks options are perceived as an entitlement, they lose their impact.

While many entrepreneurs define the edge as financial, it takes a lot more than money to succeed. For many entrepreneurs, money is a way to keep score, to gauge what other people think your company is worth, hence to establish its value. But it's not the money, per se, but what you do with it that will make or break your company. Money enables you to hire people, develop products and services that customers want, create new marketing programs, create a good work environment for your people, or build production facilities. Not all money is equal. Look for smart money. Determine how much money you need, then decide whether to go for debt or equity financing, then find the bankers, corporate partners, angel investors, or equity investors who will support your dream and share your values.

As difficult as that may seem, getting the money is the easy part. Spending it wisely, planning, hiring the right people, building an organization to support growth, and placing your bests on products, services, and market niches—that's the hard part. That's what will test your mettle as a leader.

Top Ten Lessons in Money

1. Keep your overhead as low as possible and your fixed costs to a minimum during start up and initial growth. Maintain as much flexibility as you can through contracts and out-sourcing.

2. While most companies lose money during start-up, control the burn rate and focus on generating revenue as quickly as possible.

3. Make sure your business model works. It's not about how many customers want free samples, but how many will pay. It's not about increasing revenues if expenses are out of control. It's all about profit and getting a return on your investment of time, energy and money.

4. Develop plans and budgets. Establish a trigger point (it can be expressed in time or dollars) that will require you to stop, re-evaluate the situation, and assess the prospects for growth.

5. Spread the risks and seek multiple investors, customers, and suppliers.

6. Qualify your customers and make sure they are able to pay their bills. If there's any doubt, insist on partial payment, up front, and stay on top of receivables.

7. Set up checks and balances in your company to deter employees who might try to embezzle. Have different people handling accounts payable and receivables, get regular financial reports, and schedule periodic audits.

8. Develop a relationship with one or more bankers—before you need funding. Share your business plan. Provide regular updates on progress, discuss new clients and projects. Don't wait until you need money to approach the bank.

9. Understand what options you have to finance growth. Only a small percentage of companies will interest venture capitalists so don't waste a lot of time if you don't have a high growth company with proprietary technology or a killer application. Understand the pros and cons of debt and equity financing, and strategic partnerships. Learn what kinds of financial plans and reports each will want you to provide.

10. While you may always try to get more capital than you need, once you have it, be very frugal with the money. Don't throw money at a problem. Hire good people, communicate and keep your company aligned, and execute well.

SECTION 5

≈ Personal Issues ≈

Section-at-a-Glance

Overview

Individual Profiles

Profile: James Fierro
The Edge: Lost control of his company, borrowed to the max personally, his wife left him, and he developed a rare form of cancer.

Profile: Parvinder Singh
The Edge: Success went to his head; he disregarded his family, his finances, and his business, and almost lost it all.

Profile: Bill Lee
The Edge: Was fired by his mentor; abandoned by his friends

Profile: Louette Glabb
The Edge: Partner embezzled money, swindled customers, and invested the company's cash in a bad stock. Company nearly failed.

Profile: Isaac Rosenberg
The Edge: Was kidnapped, and held hostage for four months. Later
he faced a shut-down of his distribution network after September 11.

Profile: Laura McCann
The Edge: Merged a then-successful company into a money-bleeding enterprise that failed.

Profile: Barrett Ersek
The Edge: Company burned to ground and all records were lost. Owner was juggling debt and an IRS lien for nonpayment of taxes.

Wrap-up

Top Ten Lessons in Personal Issues

≈ Personal Issues ≈
Overview

So far, you've read stories and lessons about leadership, people, partnerships, and money. Good leadership can make—or break—a company, and you've learned some of the do's and don'ts from those who shared leadership with a partner. You've learned some of the ways entrepreneurs solve their money problems and that the right people with the right direction can propel a company's growth.

While all of our stories have a personal dimension, the stories in this section provide insights about the emotional edge that entrepreneurs experience when their companies are on the brink. The picture is not always a pretty one. But you'll learn how they handled the emotional roller coaster, the highs and lows of starting and growing a company. You'll learn how they dealt with discouragement, with failure, and what their entrepreneurial experiences taught them about themselves.

James Fierro lost his business, his wife, and almost lost his life after he had borrowed to the max and was then turned out of his company by his board of directors. Parvinder Singh discovered, too late, what mattered most. The more successful his business became, the less time he devoted to his wife and family, with predictable consequences. He reminds us that it's not easy to be the spouse or child of an entrepreneur—and that entrepreneurs need to make time for their family, no matter what. Bill Lee became an entrepreneur after he was fired and had a hard time getting over it until he began to experience what he called "the divine hand of intervention." Now he figures being fired was the luckiest thing that's ever happened to him. After Louette Glabb's business partner embezzled thousands of dollars from the company, she began to assess her own strengths and weaknesses and faced up to her personal demons.

Greg Levin (who was profiled in section 4 on Money) experienced a number of business setbacks, in quick succession, that were so personally devastating that he became clinically depressed. He found that business issues can have a powerful effect on personal life. He was so overwhelmed that he never went to bed for several weeks, just slept an hour or so on his couch each day–and even stopped eating.

Isaac Rosenberg's kidnapping shaped his business philosophy and helped him learn why it's important to have a positive attitude, be able to "shift gears" when adversity strikes, and to have contingency plans. When Laura McCann's second business failed, it was a life-changing experience. She didn't like certain personal behaviors that were causing these problems and felt she needed to make a clean sweep and start again. Barrett Ersek lost all his business records in a fire, was juggling 13 credit cards, at one point owed the IRS thousands of dollars, and almost gave up. These are remarkable stories of courage, faith, determination, and persistence.

These harrowing experiences became catalysts for personal growth and development. As you read the stories, think about the questions these entrepreneurs asked themselves. How would you answer them?

- Do you know how to build a company? Do you know what you're doing right and wrong?

- If you lost everything, knowing what you know now, could you build a successful company next time?

- Do you understand the stress that your choice to be an entrepreneur and a CEO creates for your family?

- Have you figured out your priorities in life? How much time do you save for yourself, your family, your community responsibilities?

- What have your business failures and edge experiences taught you about yourself, your behaviors, your strengths and weaknesses? Have you taken the time to learn from your successes and your failures?

- Have you developed contingency plans to deal with business and personal disasters?

- When you succeed, do you remember all the people who helped you succeed—and help them to be successful?

Read on and see how entrepreneurs answered these questions.

Individual Profiles

LOSING YOUR COMPANY, LOSING EVERYTHING

Factsheet

Name:	James Fierro
Title:	CEO
Company:	InfoTag Systems, Inc.
Type of Business:	Radio frequency identification systems
Location:	Vancouver, British Columbia
Annual Revenue:	undisclosed
Employees:	5
Years in Business:	Company founded 1993
The Edge:	Lost control of his company, borrowed to the max personally, his wife left him, and he developed a rare form of cancer.

The Story

A few years ago, James Fierro—who later founded HomeGrocer.com—created a company called InfoTag Systems, Inc. Fierro funded the company himself and, as many entrepreneurs do with their businesses, put everything he had on the line. It wasn't long before the owner of a publicly listed shell company who wanted to acquire a technology company and take advantage of the hot high-tech stock market approached him. But this deal—which seemed so good at the time—was the beginning of his problems.

Says Fierro, "I did the transaction with the shell; it seemed to be in very good shape, and the guys who were behind the shell had agreed to resign. We soon raised about $2 million for the business; we'd signed some incredible deals with Caterpillar and Chrysler. But instead of resigning, they approached me and said, 'Look, we could really help you with this.' And so they stayed on.

"Over the next couple of months, as I was traveling around the world setting up operations, these guys were doing all kinds of maneuvers behind my back to take control of the company. Part of that included approaching my German inventor/partner and making him a very substantial offer. They got him to cooperate to have me removed, set him up as chairman—it was a real mess. I was in a terrible position because I had raised every penny that was in the company, and I had been the key driver in getting most of the deals signed. On top of that, I had mortgaged my house and brought everybody I loved and cared about into the deal as investors. And we were just at the threshold of doing a fairly large transaction with a big U.S. broker who was going to buy out my position, which at that time was worth somewhere between $20 and $30 million. Within a few months of the shell's board getting control of my company, I was hamstrung and couldn't sell out.

"In a matter of two or three months, everything started falling apart—I mean really falling apart. I was asked to come back at the eleventh hour to try to rescue some of the financing problems because the people were saying, 'Wait a minute, where's James? He's the one we were doing the deal with.' I felt obligated to all the investors I had brought in, so I tried to help out. I actually got things back on track. But as soon as it looked like the company was doing fine, I was out again. It was just terrible. I said, 'Okay, that's it.' And I turned my back on the situation.

"About this time my wife and I began to realize we had some difficulties. All my credit cards were maxed out. I had incurred over $150,000 of debt just to keep the company going while we were waiting for another round of funding. The guys who took over my company promised that they would pay me all that money when I left, but I never saw a penny of it. My wife said 'This is not the life I wanted to marry into.' She went out and got a lawyer— one who had a full-page ad in the yellow pages with a pit bull with a big studded collar and a caption that said, 'When we bite, we don't let go.' For some reason, she thought I had all kinds of money, but the company was quickly becoming worth zero, and everything I had was in that company. I didn't even have enough money to hire a lawyer. I ended up defending myself, and the judge awarded her a massive judgment against me. I was obviously unable to pay.

"About this time, I noticed I had this bruise on my chest that wasn't going away. I went to a doctor, and he couldn't figure out what it was. Then I noticed a couple more bruises under my arms. I went back again, and this time they took a biopsy. Then they told me I had a very rare form of cancer that attacks the outer layer of the skin, and that the recommended therapy is to burn off the outer layer of skin with high-intensity radiation. I would be bed-ridden for six months—wrapped up like a mummy so I wouldn't get infected—while a new layer of the skin regenerated.

"My heart started pounding. Sweat started coming out. I had a choked up feeling. I didn't know what it was, but it was a really intense feeling. I walked out of there in tears, thinking, 'Oh my God; I can't take six months off. I can't make my bills at the end of this month. I'm devastated. My wife's left me. She's got this court order against me. What else can go wrong?'

"I finally came to terms with what I was dealing with, and it was a feeling of loss. When you are dying, it's the loss of everything in your life that is so terrible: my kids, my wife, my business, everyone that I loved and cared about.

"But over the next three months, I researched every alternative medicine that you could imagine and decided there's no way I'd go in and get my skin burned off. I figured if the cancer wouldn't

kill me, the burning would. I looked into a whole bunch of homeo-
pathic types of remedies and went on a number of different re-
gimes including parasite cleansing, vitamin therapy, wheat grass,
and some tinctures and teas. Within three months, there was no
trace of the cancer. I went back to the doctor, and he couldn't
believe it."

Fierro walked away from his company, rebuilt his finances and
personal life, and was able to move on to a new venture. But this
time, he used the lessons he had learned to make his next business
a success.

Lessons Learned

Entrepreneurs—especially in fast-growing companies—often become consumed with the business and simply ignore everything
else: their health, their own needs, and their personal relationships. James Fierro came under enormous personal pressure and
was tested to the limit by adversity. Hostile investors took his company away. He was heavily in debt. His wife left him. He discovered that he had a very unusual form of cancer that was particularly
difficult to treat. But through it all, Fierro refused to give up.

"I spent a lot of time during this period in introspection, looking at who I am and what I'm all about, what I want to do in life,
what are my core competencies, and what kinds of people I want
to work with. I decided that I had built a lot of value in InfoTag in
a very short period of time—$80 million in less than two years—
and I could do it again. The only reason it didn't work this time is
because I got involved with the wrong people. So from there on, I
became neurotic about people. The next company I built was
HomeGrocer.com, and we did that one right. We wound up selling that for millions of dollars."

Bob Shallenberger is another entrepreneur with similar insights.
Bob has started three companies: oriental rugs, real estate, and
memorabilia. "My dad went bankrupt and didn't live long enough
to get back on his feet. When he told me what happened that took

him into bankruptcy, he finished by saying, 'It was a setback.' I said 'What do you mean, a setback? You went bankrupt!' and he said, 'Listen, it's not having the money that matters; it's knowing how to get it. Unless somebody has erased my mind, I can do it again.' You could take every single penny away from me today and six months from now I'd be back in the same place because I know how to do it."

Three of the secrets of "how to do it" are courage, contacts, and persistence. Says Fierro, "No matter how difficult or how impossible a situation seems, the only way to be sure that you don't overcome the issues or the problems is by not trying. There's just no replacement for perseverance and commitment to an outcome because the difference between success and failure is a very, very fine line. I remember when I was at the edge thinking, 'God, I can't believe all this is happening. Are we ever going to get beyond this?' Then, when you do, you say, 'Wow. We've now had some success here.' The difference is so minuscule. It could be a day. It could be a phone call."

While Fierro trusted himself and his abilities, it wasn't until he had the experience with InfoTag that he recognized the importance of surrounding himself with people he could trust. "People are really critical to the success of a venture, but it's their integrity that's most important. You just can't trust everybody. I hate to say it—deep down inside you want to be able to trust people—but not everyone is as ethical as you might be. This means that it's very important to get things in writing; handshakes and verbal agreements are not enough. If I had had the proper written documentation in place when the board began the process of ousting me from the company, it would have been impossible for them to have done it."

THE YOUNG AND THE RESTLESS

Factsheet

Name:	Parvinder Singh
Title:	Managing Director
Company:	Valley Holdings Pte. Ltd.
Type of Business:	Restaurants
Location:	Singapore
Annual Revenue:	$2.5 million (SGD)
Employees:	30
Years in Business:	Company founded 1992
The Edge:	Success went to his head; he disregarded his family, his finances, and his business, and almost lost it all.

The Story

After a short career as an information technology manager, Parvinder Singh developed a number of restaurants and bars located throughout Asia, including Singapore, Jakarta, Shanghai, and even in Mongolia. As his business grew, he spent more and more time enjoying the fruits of his labors and less and less time with his wife and children. Singh soon found that there was a high price to pay.

"I was once married to a New Zealander named Lisa. We have two kids—two boys. Lisa was a fashion designer who had moved to Singapore. When I first met her, she had just won the young designer award in New Zealand. One day I was reading the Sunday paper and I saw an ad for a space to rent in Holland Village. I paid a down payment for the rent, drove home, and told Lisa. My heart was beating really fast because I had never done anything like that before. The rent was something like 8,000 Singapore dollars a month and my salary was like 4,000 or 5,000 dollars a month. And we thought, 'How are we going to pay for this?'

"We started our first restaurant in that space in Holland Village. We brought a lot of artifacts from India—pillars, doors, windows—and we modeled our restaurant after an old Indian home. That's been the basic theme of our restaurants from then on. Word got around town about this really interesting small restaurant, and we were flooded with customers. So we opened a second restaurant, and we started making money like I've never seen before in my life. Unfortunately, I didn't handle my success very well. I started being a bit wild, going out with my friends and coming back home late all the time; by that time we had our first son. After months of this, my wife became a lot more quiet and stopped asking me when I would be coming home.

"And then I met a woman—I had an affair. That broke up my marriage, and Lisa and I split up. The split was a long, drawn-out one. It took a whole year. During this time, sales from our businesses started plummeting. I still maintained the high cost of my lifestyle and things were getting very bad. I took a mortgage out on my house to pay the bills. That was nearly half a million Singapore dollars. And then I pulled loans for another 200,000. So I borrowed 700,000. That's a lot of money. The profits were there but not enough to pay the loans. There were major cash flow issues because I had to pay the banks; otherwise, they take very strict action, taking everything including my house.

"Eventually, I realized that I needed to start hanging out with people who run their lives in a more disciplined way, people with families, with successful businesses. I'm a new man now. Just waking up on time in the morning has been a very positive change in lifestyle for me. I have sorted out my day: I fight fires in the morning, run the business (with much more attention to the numbers and the profit) in the afternoon, and then at night I go visit my restaurants. Business has picked up again, and I have paid off most of my debts.

Lessons Learned

Success as an entrepreneur can be a very heady experience, and some people handle it better than others. For many, the excitement of having more money than they could ever imagine, becoming a celebrity in the community, and attracting the attention of the public is intoxicating—and quite addictive. When Parvinder Singh's restaurants became successful, his life changed, and he soon lost control. While enjoying the fruits of his success, he forgot to manage the business and neglected his family and his personal relationships. He didn't realize the value of a stable and supportive family and home life until it was too late.

He learned another lesson: the impact of a growing company on other members of the family. "You have to understand that your family is being stretched by your activity as an entrepreneur, that you're not the only one feeling the negative effects. Many entrepreneurs think, 'I'm working hard to get this going, and they will benefit when it succeeds. They should appreciate what I am doing and not make any demands.' But just because they are members of your family does not mean they have the same resilience or tenacity that you have. Remember: *you* are the one doing this. You are the one at war, trying to create something against great odds, not them. But they want to help you and will try to support you. And you need that help and support. I've learned that you must take time out for them, no matter what."

John Younger, president of the technology company Accolo, shared a similar lesson learned. "I reached an epiphany, a very pointed, sharp, painful place when I realized that I had all the money I'd ever need, I was in great physical shape, and I was completely alone. I knew it was my own fault because I had been so driven and myopically focused on the company, but it was a horrible realization.

Thank God I had that epiphany when I was in my mid-thirties. And believe me, I have made some significant changes in my life.

"I now work to live; I don't live to work. I have a family that means more to me than anything. I recognize there are only a finite number of hours in the day and I make sure I have time with my bride and stepson. We always have dinner together, plus two hours after dinner to play and to have quality time. When I have massive deadlines—and we all do; that's part of having your own company—then I simply work later or get up earlier. I just figure out something, but not at the expense of time with them."

THE RELUCTANT ENTREPRENEUR

Factsheet

Name:	R. William Lee, III
Title:	President/CEO
Company:	Paragon Financial Group
Type of Business:	Financial Services
Location:	Atlanta, Georgia
Annual Revenue:	$5.2 million
Employees:	5
Years in Business:	Company founded 1994
The Edge:	Was fired by his mentor; abandoned by his friends

The Story

Before founding Paragon Financial Group, Bill Lee was executive vice president of a "boutique" institutional brokerage he joined in 1986. Lee quickly rose up the ranks to the position of executive vice president and seemed destined for even greater things. That is, until he received the surprise of his life from his mentor, the owner of the company.

"I was fired. I was the longest tenured person in the firm; I was the second employee that he hired. He founded the business, and I joined a team of two. It was a ground floor opportunity, and we built a very successful company. On my fifth anniversary, he did something that he'd never done before: He awarded a stock option to me. It was a 'good faith' sort of a thing, and it was ultimately for 10 percent of the company. We had a big dinner to celebrate the anniversary. He said he wanted to give me a chance to reap some of the rewards of building the business.

"The day is etched in my mind. It was July 18, 1994—a Monday—and there was no advance warning. He fired me. In retrospect, the only thing that seemed different was that there was a growing distance between us. My wife and I were celebrating our tenth anniversary in Bermuda the week before, and I remember telling her that even when I called back to the office, John wasn't available or wouldn't talk to me.

"He used to laugh and talk about when he had been at his former firm; he was quite a challenge because he was a maverick—headstrong and stubborn. He was twice divorced, in his 50s, and had a 22-year-old girlfriend. He drove around town in a red Ferrari. I was the father of two daughters, happily married, celebrating my tenth anniversary, sang in my church choir. I may be dull to a fault, but I was a good balance to him.

"Had there been warning, I could have exercised my open-ended option. But when he fired me so unexpectedly, the option just ceased to exist. That hurt a lot. In the days that followed, I made a proposal for what I considered a reasonable severance given my years of service and contributions. His response was to lob back a considerably smaller package, with a noncompete, and a nonsolicitation clause, which would have totally neutralized me. The end result was that after eight years of what he described as a 'partnership,' I was on the curb with two weeks pay.

"Fortunately, my family was tremendously supportive. My loving wife listened a lot and was very brave in those days of uncertainty. And my mom and dad were very supportive. In fact, I'll never forget when I called my father to tell him what had happened: 'Dad, you're not going to believe this, but I've just been fired.' Without missing a beat, he said, 'Great. When are we going to go into business?' Today, he is a 50/50 partner in my new business; he put up the money."

Lessons Learned

You should never take business relationships or personal relationships for granted. When you sense a change in behavior or attitude from your partner, boss, or spouse, pay attention. Acknowledge it and take time to talk with the person about it. Looking back, Bill Lee admits there were signs, but he did not address the issue with his boss when he got back from vacation. On the other hand, this experience provided some insights about life, friendships, and opportunity.

Says Lee, "I was loyal to a fault, and that left a huge blind spot in my perception of our relationship. It also kept me from seeing alternatives. I simply didn't recognize the potential of having my own business and charting my own course. If I hadn't been so loyal, I might well have left long before I was fired.

"This whole experience heightened my awareness of what I would call an unseen hand working in my life, particularly in those troubled days. The more I became aware of and in touch with that, the more I relaxed and was able to go with the flow. My faith definitely comforted me during those times, and it freed me from a lot of worry. I had a sense that somebody else was in charge and, in essence, was calling the shots, that it was not all up to me.

"In the days after I got fired, there were people who would not take my calls, people I thought were friends—businesspeople and clients. But at the same time, I was absolutely thrilled by the people who came out of the woodwork—people I never would have predicted—who offered me encouragement and assistance. When the chips are down, you really learn who your friends are, and it is surprising on both sides. There were some people who thought highly of me but didn't think highly of the firm or my boss. The minute I left the firm, they were there. Never forget who is there for you in your hour of need.

"Finally, I learned that you cannot allow yourself to be consumed by a negative experience like the one I went through. In my case, the injustice and the mistreatment that I received were incredibly unfair and abhorrent, compared to the service I had provided and the confidence I had enjoyed. I dwelled on it far too much, and people got tired of hearing about it. Eventually, a very kind older gentlemen pulled me aside, put his hand on my shoulder, and said, 'Bill, this happened to you, it's over, and people don't want to hear the gory details. Get on with your life.' Life got a lot better for me once I stopped dwelling on the past and started focusing on the future.

"Today, I have a successful, growing, profitable business, and I've got great clients and great people. I am just blessed beyond all belief to have the freedom of traveling with my family, serving on charity boards, flying my airplane, and sailing my sailboats. It's a wonderful life. If I had stayed on at the other company, I don't think my life would have been anything like this."

AN INSIDE JOB

Factsheet

Name:	Louette Glabb
Title:	President
Company:	Duplication Masters
Type of Business:	CD-Rom replication
Location:	Santa Ana, California
Annual Revenue:	$1.5 million
Employees:	10
Years in Business:	Company founded 1992
The Edge:	Partner embezzled money, swindled customers, and invested the company's cash in a bad stock. Company nearly failed.

The Story

In 1992, Louette Glabb and a business partner started Duplication Masters, a company that specializes in CD-Rom replication for software companies, high-tech companies, and marketing firms. She and her partner had been sales representatives for another company. When she decided she could do a better job than the company she was with, she quit, started her company, and convinced him to join her. Glabb thought that inviting a trusted co-worker to join her in her new venture would be a great way to build a new business, but she learned that even trusted friends don't always make trustworthy business partners.

Says Glabb, "We started off as a diskette duplication company in '92. In 1997 I asked my partner to leave because he was embezzling money. It seemed that he had a sense of entitlement to the money and just started writing personal checks—checks from the company's corporate account—for personal things. I went on vacation to Europe for five weeks and by the time I got back we had lost several good customers. Our customers told me my partner mistreated them. These were good accounts, our bread and butter, the companies that kept us in business.

"One customer said my partner had failed to return phone calls. Another said that he held their products, claiming that they were past due on a payment when they really weren't. She said, 'We pay all of our bills. Our bills are current with you. He claimed we were past due, held our shipment, and we missed our ship date. It really messed us up—it put us in a huge bind. He wouldn't listen to us, he wouldn't talk to us, he wouldn't return our phone calls, and he wouldn't deliver.' One of my personal accounts that I had grown told me, 'If you had been gone one more week, I doubt that we would ever have done business with you again.' I came very close to losing them, but I got them back. Unfortunately there were a lot of others I never did get back. A lot of them just disappeared.

"So, based on that information, I asked him to leave. Then I started going through the books—he handled all the financials. I reviewed all the numbers and saw that he was embezzling money. When I told him I was going to do an audit on the company, I never saw him again. He let me buy him out for $50,000 because he didn't want me to file charges against him.

"One thing that I know for sure was that he took $100,000 and put it into a stock fund. He called it the company stock account, but he was taking money out of that account and putting it into his personal account. He took $40,000 out of the company account, and he put it into a personal stock account that grew only he knows how much. And then he put all the money that was left in the company's corporate account into one stock. That's unheard of. And we lost it.

"He did all that behind my back. I was completely unaware that we had $100,000 in an account, that he moved money into his personal account, and that the company's money was invested in one stock. I thought we had at least $20,000 in the savings account, but he had been taking funds out of our savings and putting them into this stock account—and then he lost it all.

"It was horrible. The company was already struggling because we were transitioning from diskettes to CDs and we weren't quite into CDs yet, but the diskette business was dying. We needed the money more than ever that year to make the transition, but he was hoarding all the cash. It was really bizarre. After he left in October, we hit record numbers for the next three months. When I bought him out in January he had no idea how much money the company had made in those last three months or that it was worth $1.6 million."

Lessons Learned

Glabb used this personal disappointment and financial disaster as a wake-up call and a chance to learn more about herself.

"This experience really made me take a hard look at myself, at what kind of personality I had, at my strengths, weaknesses, and my shortcomings. I had to face the fact that I had a lot of fears. I was afraid of being strong, so I looked for a partner or hired managers who would stand up to people and be strong. That quality didn't necessarily make them good partners or employees. And that realization forced me to become a stronger person, to learn how to stand up to people, to be more confrontational, to be very direct and intentional. It also made me a lot more diligent about tracking the finances of my company."

Glabb also turned to prayer to help with the stress she was experiencing. "At first I would pray, 'Please, God. Just help us make ends meet. Just help us pay the bills.' And I got exactly what I asked for. I got just enough to pay the bills. Then I read a book, *The Prayer of Jabez*, and it said to ask for a blessing, a blessing in deed, like "Bless me. Bless me in deed and expand my territory and keep your hand upon me and keep me from evil that I may do no harm." So I started praying that prayer, every day, because I thought to myself, 'Lord, you either need to bless us or we're done—this is too stressful.'

"I started praying towards the end of May. June and July are traditionally our worst months. We were already having a bad year and I didn't want to deal with it. I thought, 'June is going to be a horrible month. Rather than sit around here while it's slow and watch us lose money, I'm going to go to Washington and do some market research.' The minute I left, the company hit production capacity, and we made more money in the month of June than we made in the prior six months put together. It was phenomenal. We made $50,000 profit in June—$50,000. My employees were so excited they could hardly stand it. They called me and said 'You're not going to believe it. We are so busy, we're working over-time.' They were so happy because they were afraid that I'd have to lay them off. It was truly a miracle."

What enabled Louette Glabb and her company to come back from the edge? Was it her faith, her sense that she was not in this alone, as Bill Lee also found, that some unseen hand was at work? Or was it her recognition of her strengths and weaknesses that led her to become a better manager and leader? Or was it because she refused to give up and remained committed to her company? With this newfound strength and commitment, Glabb was able to res-cue her company from the brink and bring it back to health and growth again.

LEARNING TO SHIFT GEARS

Factsheet

Name:	Isaac Rosenberg
Title:	President/Chief Visionary Officer
Company:	Baci Fresh
Type of Business:	Produce import/export
Location:	Pompano Beach, Florida
Annual Revenue:	$15 million+
Employees:	not disclosed
Years in Business:	Company founded 1995
The Edge:	Was kidnapped, and held hostage for four months. Later he faced a shut-down of his distribution network after September 11.

The Story

Isaac Rosenberg started Baci Fresh eight years ago. His company contracts with growers of 10 to 12 different kinds of produce in Central and South America, brings the produce to the states, then ships it to supermarket chains, food services, and wholesalers.

"My family is from Colombia and we used to manufacture soap. That was our family's business for 40 years. I was 26 years old and about to get married when I was kidnapped and held captive for four months. I missed my wedding. People didn't know if I was alive or dead. I was tied up to a tree, blindfolded, and slept outside in a little cave in the mountains.

"People ask me how I was able to cope with the kidnapping without going crazy. I was held in very rough conditions. I wasn't mistreated, but I wasn't able to take a shower in four months. I didn't have a bathroom, and I was blindfolded. I didn't say, 'Why me? Why me?' Every day I woke up thinking I was going to get released. You always have to focus on the good things that might happen, and you have to go on. I just accepted it. In business you do the same. When bad times occur in business, you have to change gears. You have to learn how to change gears and go on."

Rosenberg eventually was freed. He sold the family business and moved to the United States, where he ended up applying his importing skills to the produce industry. But that wasn't the end of his troubles.

"The September 11 disaster had a major impact on our business. We bring in a lot of produce through New York. When the World Trade Center was attacked, we had shipping containers in the water going to New York. We immediately called the container companies and the freight companies, and we diverted everything down here to Miami. There weren't any airplanes flying for four or five days, and we bring in a lot of produce through air. There was nothing we could do about it.

"Then we sat down and said, 'What happens if another disaster happens to us—maybe a bomb, or a fire in the office that destroys our records? How do we recover?' So we now have a contingency plan concerning how to proceed in case something like that happens again."

Lessons Learned

Isaac Rosenberg has learned that there are some things you can control and others you can't. If you can maintain your optimism and belief that things will get better, if you can shift gears, you can get through almost any situation. But in addition to playing the cards you are dealt, you need to think ahead, get prepared, and develop contingency plans so your company can survive a disaster.

Says Rosenberg, "I learned that sometimes in life things come to a stop, and you can't do anything about it. And then you have to start again. You never know what the day is going to bring. I believe the kidnapping prepared me for an event like the September 11 tragedy. Or when I heard my mother had cancer. When you get the initial news, it's devastating. But you have to know how to change gears and adapt to the situation."

Bob Shallenberger, the owner of an oriental rug company in St. Louis, shares a similar perspective. "We are one of the largest independent rug dealers in the country and September 11 has affected our business on all fronts. The economy was slowing down to begin with; then September 11 stopped it. I do business directly with Pakistan and Afghanistan. We had weavers making rugs in Afghanistan. I don't know where those people are, but they sure aren't hanging around in Afghanistan making rugs anymore. We had rugs ordered that we'll never see, and people we'll never talk with again. About 95 percent of the rugs in the United States go through New York City. On September 11 my suppliers lost contact with everyone. Bringing rugs through U.S. customs has gone from a four- to five-day process to a four- to five-week process. And that's money, interest, and disgruntled customers that we can't do anything about."

However, as Isaac Rosenberg discovered, you can—and should—attempt to create contingency plans to address possible worst-case scenarios. A company needs several types of contingency plans, centered on some simple questions.

What happens if our operations are interrupted for a long time?

This is clearly what happened to Bob Shallenberger's and Isaac Rosenberg's companies after September 11. But it could happen to any company if there was a fire, a strike, or a transportation catastrophe.

How do we get in touch with our key people?

You need to know how to get in touch with all of your employees, during and after working hours, and when they are traveling on company business. If there is a company emergency, or some kind of disaster affecting your business, you need a plan to communicate quickly and efficiently to keep them informed and safe. Include a description of the regular communication channels for customers, suppliers, investors, and partners in your plan as well.

What happens if the IT network gets hacked or collapses?

Devise a plan addressing network and IT security, including short-term and long-term back-up plans.

How can I keep my employees safe?

Put a plan together that goes above and beyond a fire drill. You need a plan to evacuate customers or employees from a building or workplace in case of fire, a bomb scare, and other disturbances that threaten the health or welfare of the people in your workspace.

How do we deal with faulty products?

This plan should cover concerns about product malfunction, spoiled products, product tampering, or other situations when you need to do a massive product recall. This requires dealing with the end customer through mass media as well as the supply chain customers who are distributing the product as well as your employees.

Entrepreneurs pride themselves in being able to "deal with the unexpected"—but sometimes the unexpected requires massive resources and has an impact on many more people than just you. Part of the responsibility of the leader is to manage resources carefully, and that includes people, money, customers, and "the brand." With so much at stake, don't try to "wing it." A contingency plan enables you to anticipate, think through, and be prepared for some of the most likely crises your company will face. Being able to change gears is important, but having a contingency plan will enable you to avoid the edge.

MERGING WITHOUT LOOKING BOTH WAYS

Factsheet

Name:	Laura McCann
Title:	CEO
Company:	Fashion Express Worldwide
Type of Business:	Fashion industry
Location:	New York, New York
Annual Revenue:	$39 million
Employees:	65
Years in Business:	Company founded 1992
The Edge:	Merged a then-successful company into a money-bleeding enterprise that failed.

The Story

Before Laura McCann started her current company, Z-Weave, she owned a company called Fashion Express Worldwide, which made clothes for Victoria's Secret, The Limited, and others. After buying out her partners, McCann merged her company with another company but found the synergies were simply not there. In fact, it was a disastrous move—and the company failed.

Says McCann, "I started my first company with a $20,000 loan from my dad. I had two partners who, between them put in about $160,000. We bought one partner out six months later; the remaining partner and I stayed on and grew the company to about

$40 million. So we had a nice run. We stayed together until about '97 when my partner was ready to move on, so I bought the business from him. I stayed on my own for about six months and was introduced to a couple of people who were in a similar industry space, and we put our two companies together in '97. Within two years, the company started bleeding cash, and that became very difficult, so I had to close it down in '99.

"The business failed through a combination of different factors. When we put the two companies together, one plus one didn't equal two. A lot of our operating costs were not brought down to the levels we expected. At the time, we did business in the United States, and we were an intermediary for factories. A lot of our clients consolidated and wanted to eliminate that middle person, so we had to open an office in Hong Kong. Soon we were duplicating efforts in New York and in Hong Kong. And the cost of getting that Hong Kong office off the ground was much higher than we thought. So that hurt us. When some of our customers went bankrupt, we could not get on top of it.

"There was a lot of discord between my two partners and me. Instead of going into the deal fifty-fifty—which was where we started—we each ended up with a one-third split, and I quickly lost much of my ability to direct and control the business. My business was more mature; we were the ones who had a line of credit, and we had much more infrastructure. Although these two guys were excited about putting the two companies together, they really didn't have the operating experience to do it right. They made a lot of mistakes, and I wasn't able to rein them in. For me, it became a loss of power and control.

"It was very hard on me. I really believed that we were a team working toward the same goal, but when it finally ended it was obvious that they were working against me. I surrendered a lot of my day-to-day involvement in the organization. But taking my eye off the ball really cost me. I personally lost over a million dollars.

"This experience made me take a much closer look at my entire life, and I made a couple of big decisions. One was that I wanted to change what I was doing, the business I was in. The other was I looked at my marriage and saw that there were some things that weren't working. So I closed the business, separated from my husband, sold my house, moved from the suburbs back to the city, and started all over again. I felt that a lot of what had happened was because of certain lessons that I needed to learn. One of those lessons was not to be in relationships that don't support my succeeding. The business failure was a real wake-up call, and it forced me to take a look at myself and make some very hard choices. I decided I had to make a clean sweep because the behaviors I was seeing in myself were not going to get me where I wanted to go, long term. I had to start all over again."

Lessons Learned

Entrepreneurs have an amazing resilience and ability to cope with this thing called "failure." Like the cowboy on a bucking bronco, they stay on as long as they can, and when they get bucked off, they get up, dust themselves off, and get ready to ride again. They become consumed with how they can get back on the horse because that's when they feel most alive. For most entrepreneurs, the question is not *if* they will succeed, but *when* they will succeed. They know, deep down inside, that success is right around the corner—the next horse, the next customer, the next company.

But when Laura McCann got bucked off, she began to question the whole process, including herself and how success is measured. She took time to reflect on what had led to her "failure"—why she got bucked off. When her business didn't turn out the way she expected, she looked at herself and what she was doing that led to this failure. Then she made changes in her personal and business life and moved ahead. For McCann, success is more of a journey than a destination, and failure is one of the stops along the way.

"The whole theme or concept of failure is one I've thought a lot about. As entrepreneurs, I don't think we're taught how to deal with failure, but it happens a lot. I say, 'My business failed, and I guess my marriage failed, too.' But I don't like that word. I have a lot of trouble with that word, failure. I could intellectualize and rationalize and look at all the things that were right and good that came out of those failures. But deep down inside, the words kept coming back. 'I failed. I failed.'

"I'm not sure I've found the solution of how to deal with failure. Maybe success helps you get over the failures. I'm definitely hoping that success makes me feel it's all been worth it. But I'd like to find something more—I'm not sure of the word—maybe it's spiritual. Part of going through the past two years has been my looking inside and trying to understand why things happened to me, what I did that made them happen, and what part my higher vision of myself has to do with that. I have a vision of who I think I am and what I can do. I believe that part of tapping into that vision is trusting your place in the world, and then being tuned in to all of your potential as a person. A lot of it is about giving and loving and accepting. I guess that's why I called it 'spiritual.'"

OUT OF THE ASHES

Factsheet

Name:	Barrett Ersek
Title:	Managing Partner
Company:	Custom Care Lawn Service
Type of Business:	Lawn care
Location:	Philadelphia
Annual Revenue:	$5 million
Employees:	20
Years in Business:	Company founded 1989
The Edge:	Company burned to ground and all records were lost. Owner was juggling debt and an IRS lien for nonpayment of taxes.

The Story

Barrett Ersek started working for ChemLawn when he was 12. When he was 17 he decided there was a market for a greener type of lawn service and started his own company.

"I started the company when I was a junior in high school. That year, I got 50 customers and thought I was a big shot. I ran the business when I was a junior and senior in high school and thought I'd continue it in college. My business seemed to be more exciting than college, so I dropped out before I finished the first semester.

This was not the politically correct thing to do, because my father had a Ph.D., and my brothers and sisters had master's degrees. But I focused on the business, got 300 customers, married my high school sweetheart, had a child right away, and really put my nose to the grindstone.

"Then, when I was 20, my house burned down to the ground. My office and all my records were on the third floor of the house. I was renting the house and had no insurance of any kind, and the guy who had the house didn't have insurance. It was November, the onset of winter when the lawn care business is basically idle for three months. I tried to remember where my customers lived. I went to their house, knocked on the door, and explained my situation. I asked them if they were my customers, if they owed me money—if so how much, and what I used to charge them. The response I got was amazing. When one customer offered to pay me for the next year's lawn care, I wrote all of them and offered a discount if they would pay in advance.

"I raised the money to get through the winter, got another house, and really focused on marketing. I spent my profits just to get through the winter and do all this marketing. But I figured if I could double the business, I'd have enough. I got good at demographics and tracking the results of customer marketing.

"By the time I was 22, we were back on top and life was good. I had bought a house, the business was growing 50 to100 percent, and I had the marketing figured out. But I didn't have the cash flow figured out, so the business was growing faster than the cash flow could support it. I figured as long as I was selling and growing, I'd be making money. I was making money on paper, but it was never in my bank account until 30, 60, even 90 days later. I ended up making payroll with credit cards. At one point, I was juggling back and forth between 15 credit cards to make payroll and keep everything paid. I couldn't figure it out; I had no idea what was going wrong. I didn't want to tell anybody about the problem because I thought maybe I was failing, and I didn't want anyone to know I was failing, so I kept it all inside and tried to figure it out.

"In the meantime, I had stopped paying taxes because payroll and other things seemed more urgent, and I figured I'd pay them later. Next thing I know, it's three years later and the IRS is putting a lien on my personal property for back income taxes, sales taxes, payroll taxes. One day, I've got $10,000 in the bank, and the next day I've got nothing but a huge debt to the IRS.

"We went down to bare, bare bones, didn't spend any money on marketing, and just tried to put as much of the money as possible into paying down all this debt. By the end of three years, I was beat up, torn up, sick of being in business for myself, sick of the lawn care business, done. So I put the business on the market, and when they offered me $400,000, I said to myself, "Hey! This is stupid. If this company is worth $400,000 now, I could turn it into a $1 million business. Then I'll sell it for $1 million and that'll be enough to do anything I want.' My new goal was to become a $1 million company in three years, with no debt.

"We reached our goal in two years, instead of three, and I said, "This is fun. We're making a lot of money. I don't owe any money. Why would I ever want to sell this business?" So I got refocused and re-energized. When one of my employees said he was thinking of starting his own lawn care business, I said, 'Let's start up a franchise, and I'll help you. You can use all my experience, we'll take a piece of the action, and you'll do better and we'll do better.' So that's what we did.

"And now we're about a $5 million company. We have five locations; the core business did $2.5 million, the franchises combined did another $1 million, we've opened up a new company-owned location that did close to $1 million in sales, and we're in the process of setting up two new franchises and looking at a third company-owned location."

Lessons Learned

One of the most important lessons Ersek learned was the way money flows through the company. "I've learned a lot about cash flow and managing cash flow; the importance of budgeting, planning your money, and looking at statements on a regular basis. We put together a budget at the beginning of the year and then monitor it on a weekly, sometimes daily, basis. We run cash flow reports, do profit and loss statements, and we now have good marketing models and expense models. We know who our average customer is, how long it takes the customer to pay, and how much bad debt we're going to have. When we get new customers, we plug in the numbers and they flow right through; the model shows me how much cash we're going to have, when we're going to get it, and how much cash we'll need to bridge between now and then. I used to think, 'I don't have enough money. I've got to sell more lawns.' But the more I sold, the deeper in debt I got. As strange as it sounds, I had to stop growing the business for 3 years—to get out of debt.

"The second lesson I learned is to pay taxes first. It's terrible to be beholden to the IRS. It was one of the worst experiences of my life, and I didn't tell anybody. I didn't tell my accountant or lawyer. I felt like a failure, so I just dealt with it on my own. I paid all the penalties and interest and everything. My advice to anyone else in that situation is to get your lawyer and accountant involved early.

"A third lesson I learned is to get involved with a peer group. I was 22 years old, owned my own business, had a family—and was like a freak of nature. There wasn't anybody like me. My dad was a schoolteacher. I couldn't talk with him about this stuff. So there wasn't anybody for me to talk to, and it was hard. Today, I'm in YEO (Young Entrepreneurs' Organization) and that's been an invaluable resource to help me continue to grow my business.

"One of the guys was able to help me put together a legitimate business plan. We went to the bank and got a $400,000 line of credit at an interest rate of one point over prime. It changed my world. I didn't think I could get a $30,000 line of credit. It was just a matter of presenting the right kind of plan and explaining the business properly—but I couldn't have done it without the resources of my peer group.

"My fourth lesson is that employees want opportunities to work hard, have fun, and share in the rewards. Our business is very labor-intensive, so labor is a huge issue for all the lawn care companies. While my competitors were complaining that they couldn't grow their business because they couldn't get people to work for them, we grew 50 percent and did not put one ad in the classified section. The reason we were able to grow like this is because we communicate a vision, and our goal is to create opportunity for all our employees—through growth. We also do a lot of fun things as a group: fishing, rock climbing, and sporting events. So our employees tell all their friends who are doing jobs they don't like to come work for our company. And they do. And it's great!"

≈ Wrap-up ≈

The entrepreneurs we met in this section faced great adversity and challenge but persevered through it all. Some might find fighting cancer, divorce, a kidnapping, or having your home or business going up in flames to be a debilitating personal tragedy. But these individuals used these challenges as a part of making their business grow and to learn more about themselves, to reinvent their lives and companies, and to prepare for a more successful Round 2.

This unique spirit is what makes entrepreneurs special. Their drive, their ambition, their persistence in the face of adversity, and their desire to fight the good fight is an inspiration to us, and we hope, to you.

As an entrepreneur, you will be personally tested. We hope you can find strength in the strength of these individuals. We hope that their courage and resolve unlock the same within you. And although we offer our Top Ten Lessons for dealing with personal adversity, we hope that if you learn one lesson from this section it's that when you get knocked down, you can get back up.

Top Ten Lessons in Personal Issues

1. Don't take personal relationships for granted. Value your family and friends as much as your business. Understand that your family may not have the same goals as you.

2. Do some due diligence on people you work with, including partners, investors, employees, and even customers.

3. Address fears and concerns promptly. Your intuition was good enough to get you this far—don't ignore it now. Check into things that might be potential problems. Recognize changes in behavior, attempts to cover up, tensions among team members, and problems at home.

4. Keep your ears open. Don't ignore any aspect of your business. It's your responsibility to know what's going on. Learn to do this by tracking key performance indicators and talking with a variety of different people in the company.

5. Remember your personal investments are more than just money. Take care of your health and your stress levels.

6. Focus on your business, not your success. Focusing on success often leads people to forget about business.

7. Seek inspiration from a variety of sources. Some find answers from partners and mentors, others from their faith.

8. Find a mentor or a peer group and discuss your problems with them, rather than talking about business problems with your top team, your spouse, children, family members, or employees. Talking with peers often relieves stress, enables you to solve problems, and reminds you that you are not alone in the problems you are facing.

9. Separate your personal finances and your business finances as much as possible. As quickly as possible pay off your credit cards, get the bank to remove personal guarantees, and make sure your personal life is not destroyed if, for some reason, the business fails.

10. Remember, the Edge does not equal the End. Always try to save the company, even reinvent it if possible, but don't be afraid to walk away from problems that are beyond your ability to impact or control. There are always new doors to open, and another journey to begin.

≈ Conclusion ≈

We hope these stories have not only inspired you but have taught you how to avoid the edge. And if you are on the edge, this book should enable you to recognize that and think through what your options are. If you have read the book straight through, you may be in overload with "lessons learned." Step back for a moment and think about the most common themes that enabled each entrepreneur to get back from the edge: courage, persistence, innovation, survival skills, support from peers and family, and the ability to reinvent the company. And it should be no surprise that all entrepreneurs in our stories demonstrated ethical behavior and honest dealings with partners, vendors, suppliers, customers, bankers, financiers, and employees.

So, now what do you do—besides read this book again?

Your next step should be to join a peer group. The entrepreneurs in this book mentioned the importance of a peer group many times. It really helps to have a peer group of fellow entrepreneurs to talk with and learn from. It's a great way to get help solving your problems and leap-frog your learning. Most entrepreneurs find it difficult to share their worst fears and problems with their spouse, partner, banker, venture capitalist, or board members. You need an impartial group of people who will serve as your own personal board of advisors, which is a different role from the one your company's board of directors must play. The people on your "personal board" would ideally be people who have tried or are trying to build a company and who have recently faced or are currently going through the same issues as you are.

Having a mentor—or mentors—can also be very helpful to you. Mentors are people outside of your peer group who are more experienced in building companies and who can help guide you and share "wisdom" based on their years of real-world experience. While people on your company's board might have the qualities and qualifications to be a mentor, recognize that their fiduciary responsibilities may preclude them from serving as mentors. One of their roles is to sit in judgment of your performance to assure all stakeholders that the company has the very best leadership possible. Some board members may be reluctant to mentor you, because they'll want to stay focused on measuring your performance.

Most of the people profiled in this book are or have been a member of the Young Entrepreneurs' Organization (YEO) or its alumni organization, World Entrepreneurs' Organization (WEO). YEO and WEO are membership organizations of approximately 5,000-plus entrepreneurs all over the world.

A number of other organizations also encourage the formation of peer groups and use of mentors, including CEO Club, Inc., FastTrac, Inner Circle International, The Executive Committee (TEC), Women Presidents' Organization, Renaissance Executive Forums, and others that operate on a regional or local level. Each of these groups has its own unique membership requirements, but they all welcome new members who meet their criteria. Go to the Web or contact a local chapter in your area for more information about these and other support organizations.

In addition to joining a peer group and finding a mentor, be sure to check out some of the many excellent resources available to entrepreneurs on the Web. Two of our favorites are these:

- EntreWorld (www.entreworld.org): Sponsored by the Ewing Marion Kauffman Foundation, EntreWorld bills itself as "a world of resources for entrepreneurs." At this Web site, you'll find extensive information about starting and growing a business, articles of interest to entrepreneurs—written by experienced entrepreneurs and Top Advisors—Quickfacts, downloadable tools, expert advice, a bookstore, and much, much more.

- Edward Lowe Peerspectives (www.peerspectives.org): Sponsored by the Edward Lowe Foundation, Peerspectives offers a wide variety of resources to entrepreneurs, including a monthly E-newsletter chock-full of topical articles, and insights on issues of interest to "second stage" entrepreneurs—those trying to grow a business. Unique to Peerspectives is a peer group directory to facilitate the linking up of entrepreneurs with groups of peers in their geographical area.

Check out M.B.A. or Executive Education programs that are designed to help entrepreneurs grow. Look for programs that include peer-to-peer learning as well as faculty lectures and expert presentations. Babson College has some of the highest-rated programs, but Wharton at the University of Pennsylvania; Kellogg at Northwestern; Darden at the University of Virginia; the Sloan School at MIT; the University of Southern California; University of Colorado, Boulder; and the University of Texas, Austin, all have very strong programs focused on entrepreneurship.

Be sure to look for local programs specifically designed to meet the needs of local communities of entrepreneurs. For example, the Helzberg Entrepreneurial Mentoring Program in Kansas City was able to link young, first-time entrepreneurs with experienced entrepreneurs and business executives in Kansas City, and this produced some amazing growth in those young companies. In Dallas/ Fort Worth, the North Texas Commission (NTC) Mentor-Entrepreneur Program works to improve the local economy by developing the capabilities of minority and women owners of small businesses. In South Bend, Indiana, the Notre Dame Entrepreneurs Club recently kicked off a series of networking dinners to bring aspiring student entrepreneurs together with successful local and alumni entrepreneurs. While there are many programs that could help you, get involved in programs where *you* can help other entrepreneurs. Bottom line: Get involved, learn, and help others learn.

The fifty-plus entrepreneurs profiled in this book have told you their stories. And we have tried to translate these stories into actionable lessons that you can immediately put to work in your business and personal lives. But now it's your turn.

It's your turn to step up to your responsibilities as leader of your company. It's your turn to learn more about financing strategies, to study the pros and cons of each, and to put in good financial systems to protect your investment. Remember: It's your money, time, and effort that are being invested, so protect your investment. It's your turn to recruit and hire the very best people you can, people who can help you grow; then learn how to delegate effectively so they can help you manage and lead your company. It's your turn to develop, market, and sell innovative products and services that make a real difference in people's lives. It's your turn to demonstrate—by what you say and do—the importance of the highest standards of personal ethics and excellence. It's your turn to make something from nothing and to create a business that is built to last, a legacy that will long outlive you.

It's your turn to take these lessons and to do great things with them.

Learn how to avoid the edge, whenever possible. But if you find yourself there, you need to know how to get back and how to move on. Have the courage to take risks. Dare to try, know the odds, and be prepared to live with the consequences. Not every entrepreneur and business owner will be successful. But the absence of success is not the same as "failure." Very few entrepreneurs believe they have failed—even when their business has not succeeded. In their minds, they just ran out of time or money, or they couldn't find enough customers soon enough. If entrepreneurs are anything, they are resilient; they learn their lessons from the edge and they are sure that if they can have just one more chance, they will be successful.

As legendary football coach Vince Lombardi once remarked, "We didn't lose the game, we just ran out of time."

But if you ever do go over the edge, learn from your mistakes, reinvent your company, and bounce back. As Sam Boyer noted, we entrepreneurs always overestimate how much of our success—or failure—is within our control. So much depends on what competitors do, the markets, the weather, or the wholesale price of coffee beans! No matter how hard you work, there's a chance you won't be successful. And recent history has taught us that no matter how badly you execute, there is always a chance you will succeed. The recognition that not everything is within our control should keep us humble when we achieve success, and help us maintain our sanity when we do not.

We're pulling for you, and we wish you every success in your exciting journey. And watch out for that edge!

≈ Index ≈

Jana Matthews

Dr. Jana Matthews, founder and CEO of Boulder Quantum Ventures (www.boulderquantumventures.com), is an expert on entrepreneurial leadership and business growth. Based in Boulder, Colorado, she works with founding entrepreneurs, CEOs, corporate executives and top teams to unlock their company's growth potential. Matthews also consults with state and national governments and foundations on entrepreneurship. She is a School of Executive Education Professor at Babson College, has taught courses and guest lectured at several universities, and has designed and delivered programs to entrepreneurs and business owners in the United States, Russia, the Czech Republic, New Zealand, Australia, and the United Kingdom. Matthews has co-authored seven books, including *Leading at the Speed of Growth: Journey from Entrepreneur to CEO*, and *Building the Awesome Organization: Six Components that Drive Entrepreneurial Growth* with Katherine Catlin. She has a doctorate from Harvard University and in her spare time enjoys fly-fishing with her husband, Chuck, in New Zealand.

Jeff Dennis

Jeff Dennis is a serial entrepreneur. As a co-founder of Flagship Capital Partners, a private merchant bank, he has been involved in start-ups, acquisitions and financings for a variety of businesses in industries as varied as real estate, film and television production, insurance, cosmetics, franchising and high technology. His current project is Secutor Capital Management Corporation, which provides wealth management for high income individuals through "defensive capital management." Through his association with the Young Entrepreneurs Organization and the Ewing Marion Kauffman Foundation, he has created a series of "Lessons from the Edge" seminars. Jeff is a lawyer by training, having done his undergraduate work at Brown University and his law degree at the University of Western Ontario. He lives in Toronto with his wife Lori and their children Matt and Allie.

Peter Economy

Peter Economy is associate editor of the award-winning magazine, *Leader to Leader* and co-author of *Why Aren't You Your Own Boss?* (Prima, 2003), *Leadership Ensemble: Lessons in Collaborative Management from the World's Only Conductorless Orchestra* (Times Books, 2001), *Managing For Dummies* 2nd Edition (John Wiley and Sons, 2003), and many other books. He is the featured management expert at AllBusiness.com (www.allbusiness.com), and writes business articles for a variety of publications, including Gallup Management Journal and Sailing World. Peter Economy combines this wealth of writing experience with more than 15 years of front-line business management experience. Peter has a bachelor of arts degree with majors in economics and human biology from Stanford University and is currently pursuing MBA studies at the Edinburgh Business School. He lives in La Jolla, California.